10 PRINCIPLES FOR A LIFE OF SUCCESS AND HAPPINESS

How to Build a Fulfilling Life in a Changing World

10 PRINCIPLES FOR A LIFE OF SUCCESS AND HAPPINESS

How to Build a Fulfilling Life in a Changing World

Jean Luc Blanc and Judlie Pierre-Jacques

979-8-9939912-0-7 (Paperback ISBN)
979-8-9939912-1-4 (Hardcover ISBN)
979-8-9939912-2-1 (Ebook ISBN)

Table of Contents

CHAPTER 8

CHAPTER 9

CHAPTER 10

CONCLUSION

ABOUT THE AUTHORS

DEDICATION

This book is dedicated first and foremost to God, whose grace, wisdom, and strength have carried us through every chapter of our lives. Nothing in these pages would exist without His guidance.

To our beloved children, Gabriel and Gianni—you are our greatest inspiration. Everything we do, we do with the hope of giving you a foundation of faith, discipline, and love. Your smiles, curiosity, and joy remind us every day of the importance of building a legacy rooted in purpose and integrity.

And finally, to everyone striving to grow, to heal, and to build a meaningful life—may these words encourage you to keep moving forward with courage, clarity, and faith.

ACKNOWLEDGEMENTS

We extend our heartfelt gratitude to the people who made this journey possible.

To our families, who surrounded us with love, prayers, encouragement, and unwavering support. Thank you for believing in us, standing with us, and reminding us of the power of unity and perseverance.

To our publisher, Robin, thank you for your professionalism, your guidance, and your commitment to helping us bring our message to life. Your patience, insight, and dedication made this project smoother and stronger.

To our friends, mentors, and the wonderful community that has cheered us on throughout this process—your encouragement kept us motivated on the long nights and early mornings. We are grateful for every conversation, every reminder to stay focused, and every word of affirmation.

And most importantly, to every reader holding this book: Thank you. Thank you for giving us the honor of speaking into your life. Our prayer is that these principles guide you, strengthen you, and inspire you to pursue the meaningful, purpose-driven life you deserve.

With love and gratitude,

Jean Luc & Judlie

INTRODUCTION

A BLUEPRINT FOR
A MEANINGFUL LIFE

We live in an age of rapid change. Technology is evolving at lightning speed, economies shift overnight, and entire industries rise and fall within a decade. Even our personal lives often feel like they're spinning faster than we can manage. In this constant motion, many people feel unsettled, chasing success but never quite catching it, or pursuing happiness only to find it fading the moment they think they've grasped it.

Yet, amid this uncertainty, there is good news. Success and happiness are not accidents of birth, nor are they simply products of luck. They are built on timeless principles—principles that don't change even when the world around us does. These principles form a foundation, a solid ground beneath our feet when everything else feels unstable.

Think of it like constructing a house. No matter how beautiful the walls or impressive the design, if the foundation is weak, the structure will eventually collapse. In the same way, no matter how talented, educated, or ambitious you are, without the correct principles guiding your life, your pursuit of success and happiness

11

will crumble under pressure. Jesus Himself illustrated this in Matthew 7:24–25, when He said, "Everyone who hears these words of mine and puts them into practice is like a wise man who built his house on the rock. The rain came down, the streams rose, and the winds blew and beat against that house; yet it did not fall, because it had its foundation on the rock." *This book, 10 Principles for a Life of Success and Happiness*, is about laying that rock-solid foundation. It is about learning the timeless truths that can guide you to a life of fulfillment, no matter what storms come your way.

Throughout this journey, you will discover principles like clarity of vision, discipline, adaptability, emotional intelligence, resilience, service, and purpose. Each one will be unpacked with stories, examples, and biblical insights to show you not only *what* they are, but *how* you can live them out in your everyday life.

We didn't write this book from a place of theory alone. Our own journeys have been ones of highs and lows, victories and losses, moments of clarity and seasons of struggle. We've learned that success without joy is empty, and happiness without purpose is fragile. What truly sustains us is a life built on principles—values that shape our decisions, guide our actions, and keep us grounded when life shakes us.

Perhaps you are at a crossroads right now. Maybe you feel stuck, uncertain of your direction, or frustrated with your progress. Maybe you've experienced setbacks that have left you questioning your abilities. Or maybe you're already on a good path but sense there's more—more fulfillment, more impact, more depth—waiting for you. Wherever you are, this book is for you.

As you read, we encourage you not to rush. Reflect on each principle. Take time to do the exercises. Write in the margins. Let the lessons become personal. Because transformation does not come from reading alone—it comes from applying what you've read.

Imagine your life a year from now, five years from now, or even ten years from now. What if you were living with unshakable clarity, strong discipline, and resilience to face any challenge? What if you had not only achieved success in your career or finances but also found deep, lasting happiness in your relationships, health, and spiritual life? That is the vision of this book: to help you build a life that thrives in every dimension.

The journey begins with the first principle: clarity of vision. Before you can achieve success or find happiness, you must know where you are going. Without vision, life drifts. With vision, life becomes a purposeful adventure. So let us begin.

CHAPTER 1

PRINCIPLE 1: CLARITY OF VISION – KNOW WHERE YOU'RE GOING

"Where there is no vision, the people perish: but he that keepeth the law, happy is he."—Proverbs 29:18 (KJV)

The Power of Personal Vision

Imagine walking into a dense forest with no compass, no map, and no idea where you are going. You may move, but you will likely walk in circles, wasting energy and time, perhaps even stumbling into danger. Yet, this is how many people live their lives—busy, always on the move—but not necessarily moving *toward* something meaningful.

A personal vision is not just a goal, nor is it a list of resolutions you set at the beginning of the year and forget by February. Vision is bigger: it is the picture of your future that keeps you steady in life's storms and the "why" that keeps you moving when everything in you wants to quit. Vision gives direction, clarity, and energy.

Think of a farmer preparing a field. Without a vision of the harvest he expects, the work of plowing, sowing, watering, and weeding would feel endless and pointless. Yet, because he sees the harvest in his mind's eye before the first seed even touches the soil, he perseveres. Vision gives meaning to hard work.

The same is true in your personal life. Without a vision, you may get caught in a cycle of reacting instead of creating. Days blur into weeks, weeks into months, and before you know it, years pass by with little to show. But when you have clarity of vision—whether it's building a business, strengthening your family, growing spiritually, or improving your health—you know exactly why each step matters.

A Story of Misplaced Vision

There was once a young man who wanted nothing more than to be wealthy. He worked tirelessly, often pulling sixteen-hour days. He rarely saw his family, skipped church, and convinced himself that once he "made it," he would make it up to them. His vision was clear: accumulate money.

Years passed, and he did accumulate wealth. He bought the cars, the house, and the status symbols he had dreamed about. Yet when he looked around, he was alone. His marriage had withered, his children hardly knew him, and the peace he thought money would bring never arrived. His vision had been misplaced. He had climbed the ladder of success only to find it leaning against the wrong wall.

This story is not unique. Many people trade relationships, health, or spiritual integrity for visions built on shallow foundations. A vision without alignment to truth and eternal values can become a trap.

The good news is that misplaced vision can be corrected. Just as a ship can alter its course when it realizes it is off-track, so can we. It starts with asking the hard questions: Is my vision centered on what truly matters? Will my vision bring lasting joy and fulfillment, or only temporary satisfaction?

Clarity of vision is the foundation of a successful and joyful life. Without it, you drift. With it, you move with purpose, even when life gets tough. True vision is not selfish or shallow—it is rooted in God's truth, aligned with your deepest values, and oriented toward service, growth, and impact.

To live a life of success and happiness in a changing world, you must begin here—with vision. Write it. Refine it. Pray over it. Carry it in your heart. Because once your vision is clear, your steps will follow with confidence and strength.

CHAPTER 2

PRINCIPLE 2: DISCIPLINE AND CONSISTENCY – THE BRIDGE TO ACHIEVEMENT

"No discipline seems pleasant at the time, but painful. Later on, however, it produces a harvest of righteousness and peace for those who have been trained by it."—Hebrews 12:11

The Power of Steady Progress

Discipline is often misunderstood as something harsh, rigid, or restrictive. In reality, discipline is a form of freedom—it creates structure that allows us to focus on what truly matters. Without discipline, even the most gifted people fail to reach their potential because their talent lacks direction. Think of discipline as the framework that holds your goals together, giving them shape and stability over time. When paired with consistency, discipline becomes the steady engine that powers success.

Consistency is the quiet force that differentiates long-term achievement from short-term enthusiasm. Anyone can feel inspired for a day or motivated for a week, but lasting results require the daily commitment to show up, even when the excitement fades. Whether you want to build a career, strengthen your health, or deepen your relationships, consistency is what transforms desire into reality. The journey to happiness is not about chasing fleeting bursts of motivation but about creating steady patterns of progress.

A disciplined life teaches us to control impulses, choose what aligns with our greater vision, and stay focused when distractions call for our attention. In today's fast-paced world, distractions are everywhere, from constant notifications to the pull of instant pleasures. Discipline acts like a compass, bringing us back to what truly matters. Over time, these choices build momentum, proving that slow, steady progress outweighs momentary shortcuts.

Discipline and Consistency in Different Aspects of Our Lives

When discipline and consistency become part of our lifestyle, success stops being accidental and starts becoming intentional. Instead of waiting for the "right moment," we create the right moment by building habits that align with our vision. Each day is an opportunity to practice discipline in small ways that seem invisible at first but eventually shape the entire direction of our lives. Happiness, then, is not found in quick fixes, but in the fulfillment that comes from faithful, consistent growth.

In Relationships

Relationships thrive not on occasional grand gestures, but on steady, consistent actions over time. A single act of kindness can brighten someone's day, but consistent kindness builds trust that lasts for years. Whether in friendships, family, or marriage, consistency communicates reliability, and reliability deepens connection. People want to know they can count on you, not just once, but continually. This sense of security becomes the foundation of love and respect.

For example, a parent who consistently shows up to listen to their child after school builds a deeper bond than one who offers occasional gifts without genuine presence. A friend who checks in regularly, even with a simple message, becomes more valuable than one who appears only during crises. These steady actions may seem small, but their impact is profound. Consistency in relationships creates an environment where trust, loyalty, and love flourish naturally.

Discipline also plays a role in relationships. It takes discipline to listen rather than react, to forgive rather than hold a grudge, and to prioritize quality time in a busy schedule. In a world where it is easy to withdraw when things get hard, discipline gives us the strength to remain steady. It reminds us that love is not just a feeling, but a choice repeated every day.

Consistency in relationships is also about showing patience when others fall short of expectations. No one is perfect, and every bond faces its own set of challenges. Yet when discipline and consistency guide us, we respond with grace instead of frustration. Over time, this steady faithfulness builds connections that are not easily broken. It transforms relationships into a source of long-lasting joy and support, strengthening our pursuit of happiness.

In Finances

One of the clearest areas where discipline and consistency pay off is in our financial lives. Money, when handled without discipline, slips through our fingers faster than we realize. But when approached with consistency, even small amounts grow into wealth over time. The key is not in earning more but in making intentional, disciplined choices with what we already have.

For example, setting aside a small percentage of your income every month may not seem significant at first. Yet, over the years, that steady habit compounds into stability and freedom. This principle works whether you are saving for emergencies, investing for the future, or simply managing your daily expenses. The discipline of budgeting—choosing needs over wants—teaches us patience, while consistency ensures progress.

Financial discipline also involves resisting the urge for instant gratification. Advertisements constantly tempt us with quick pleasures: the newest phone, a luxury trip, or an impulse purchase. Discipline reminds us to pause and ask ourselves, *Does this align with my long-term goals?* Choosing growth over momentary comfort may feel difficult in the moment, but it produces lasting peace. Financial security is not built overnight, but through steady, consistent steps taken year after year.

Consistency in finances also teaches responsibility and integrity. Paying bills on time, avoiding unnecessary debt, and keeping promises in financial commitments build trust—not only with others—but also with ourselves. Over time, these habits create a sense of control and stability. Discipline and consistency in money management go beyond numbers. They become tools that allow us to live with freedom and purpose.

In Health

Your health is the foundation on which your life is built. Discipline in caring for your body ensures that you have the energy and strength to pursue your goals. Eating wisely, exercising regularly, and resting properly may seem ordinary, but these practices yield extraordinary results over time. Without good health, success in other areas becomes much harder to sustain.

The challenge is that health discipline requires consistency. Starting a diet or workout plan with excitement is easy, but continuing when progress is slow is what matters. Lasting change comes from making repeated small choices: taking the stairs instead of the elevator, drinking water instead of soda, or sleeping earlier instead of staying up late. These choices compound into long-term wellness.

Caring for your body is also an act of stewardship. When you treat your health as a priority, you honor the gift of life you have been given. Strong health not only benefits you but also allows you to serve and support others more effectively. Discipline in this area is not about perfection but about faithfulness.

In Work

In the workplace, talent may open doors, but consistency builds trust and influence. Employers value individuals who consistently show up on time, complete tasks reliably, and deliver quality results. Over time, this consistency earns respect and opportunities that natural talent alone cannot secure.

Discipline at work includes managing time effectively and staying focused on priorities. Many people struggle not because they lack skill but because they fail to control distractions. A disciplined worker who quietly and steadily delivers results often outperforms those who are inconsistent, even if they are highly talented.

Work consistency also creates a reputation that speaks louder than words. When others know they can depend on you, they are more willing to give you greater responsibilities. Career growth is often less about brilliance and more about faithfulness. By practicing discipline and consistency in your work, you build a foundation for long-term success.

The Reward of Faithful Living

Faithful living is the fruit of discipline and consistency. It is not about perfection but about showing up with steady commitment every single day. When we live faithfully—whether in our work, relationships, or personal growth—we build a life of integrity that inspires others. The reward is not just external success but inner peace—the knowledge that we are living in alignment with our values.

Happiness, in this sense, does not come from sudden breakthroughs or constant excitement. Instead, it emerges quietly from the fulfillment of knowing that each day we are moving in the right direction. Just as seeds take time to grow into trees, our daily efforts may not yield immediate results. Yet over time, those small acts of faithfulness blossom into abundance, blessing not only us but also those around us.

Faithful living also allows us to weather life's storms with resilience. When challenges arise, consistency acts as our anchor. Because we have trained ourselves in discipline, we can respond with strength rather than despair. We know that setbacks are temporary, but faithfulness endures. This mindset transforms difficulties into opportunities for growth, rather than reasons to give up.

The reward of faithful living is leaving a legacy. Discipline and consistency not only build a successful life but also set an example for others to follow. The habits we model—whether in our families, communities, or workplaces—become seeds planted in the lives of others. In this way, faithful living extends beyond ourselves, shaping a world where success and happiness are built on steady, intentional progress.

CHAPTER 3

PRINCIPLE 3: ADAPTABILITY - THRIVE IN A CHANGING WORLD

"See, I am doing a new thing! Now it springs up; do you not perceive it?"
—Isaiah 43:19

The Necessity of Adaptability

Life never stays the same for long. Circumstances shift, economies fluctuate, relationships evolve, and even our personal goals transform over time. To resist change is to remain stuck in places that no longer serve us, while the rest of the world moves forward. Adaptability is not about abandoning who you are but about adjusting to new conditions while staying anchored in your values.

Adaptability allows us to face uncertainty with courage rather than fear. Those who thrive in a changing world are not necessarily the strongest or the most intelligent— they are the ones most willing to learn and adjust. The reality is that change is inevitable, but growth is optional. By choosing to adapt, we transform challenges into opportunities and obstacles into stepping stones.

Many people fall into the trap of clinging to the past. They long for the comfort of familiarity, even when it no longer brings growth. Adaptability invites us to loosen our grip and embrace the unknown with an open heart. When we approach change as a natural part of life, we stop fighting it and begin using it as a tool for growth and progress.

Adaptability is not just about survival—it is about thriving. A flexible mindset empowers us to remain steady in our purpose while shifting our methods to fit new realities. This balance ensures that we stay relevant, resilient, and prepared for whatever lies ahead.

Seeing Change as Opportunity

The first step toward adaptability is changing the way we view change itself. Many see it as a threat, something to fear or avoid. Yet every change carries within it the possibility of growth. The shift may not feel comfortable at first, but it often opens doors we never imagined. Viewing change as an opportunity positions us to act boldly, rather than shrinking back.

Consider a career change, for example. At first, it may feel like loss—the end of security or familiarity. But within that transition lies the possibility of acquiring new skills, greater fulfillment, and broader horizons. What appears to be a setback may actually be a redirection toward something better suited for us. When we shift our perspective, change becomes less of a disruption and more of a gift.

Change also helps us shed what no longer fits. Old habits, unhelpful relationships, or outdated ways of thinking often hold us back. A shift in circumstances can expose these limitations and invite us to step into healthier, stronger versions of ourselves. Without change, we might remain trapped in cycles that limit our growth.

Seeing change as an opportunity requires faith and courage. We may not always see the benefits immediately, but by leaning into change with an open mind, we begin to recognize the hidden blessings. Instead of fearing what's uncertain, we learn to trust that new beginnings often carry the seeds of greater success and happiness.

Staying Curious and Learning Continuously

Adaptability thrives in an environment of curiosity. When we remain open to learning, we are better prepared to handle unexpected shifts. Skills that were valuable yesterday may become irrelevant tomorrow, but a curious, teachable spirit ensures we are constantly growing. Staying curious keeps us from becoming stagnant in a world that never stops evolving.

Continuous learning does not always mean formal education. It may be as simple as reading new books, observing others, asking questions, or experimenting with unfamiliar tasks. Every new skill we develop becomes another tool in our toolbox, ready for the day it is needed. The more tools we gather, the more confident we become in facing change.

Curiosity also keeps our minds flexible. Instead of clinging to one way of doing things, we become eager to explore alternatives. This mindset prevents fear from taking over when the familiar no longer works. A curious person does not panic when things shift. Instead, they see it as an invitation to discover something new.

In many ways, curiosity is a posture of humility. It acknowledges that we do not know everything and that there is always room to grow. This humility prepares us to adapt gracefully instead of resisting change with pride. By embracing lifelong learning, we develop resilience that carries us through every stage of life.

Resilience: Falling, Rising, and Adjusting

Adaptability is closely tied to resilience—the ability to recover from setbacks and keep moving forward. Life will inevitably knock us down at times. What defines us is not how often we fall but how often we rise again.

Resilience enables us to learn from failure, adjust, and emerge stronger.

Falling does not mean failure is final. It often signals that we need to change our approach, learn something new, or refine our strategy. Each setback contains valuable lessons if we are willing to look for them. Adaptable people do not let difficulties destroy their determination. Instead, they use challenges as stepping stones toward growth.

Resilience also builds inner strength. Each time we rise after a setback, we develop deeper confidence in our ability to overcome obstacles. This confidence carries into every area of life, reminding us that no challenge is too great when met with persistence and adaptability. Over time, resilience transforms difficulties into defining moments of growth.

Adjusting quickly is the final step in resilience. It is not enough to rise again—we must rise with wisdom. By learning from mistakes and adapting strategies, we avoid repeating the same errors. This cycle of falling, rising, and adjusting ensures that we are constantly moving closer to success and happiness, no matter how many times life shifts around us.

Adaptability in Relationships

Relationships are one of the greatest areas where adaptability is tested. People grow, change, and evolve over time, and a relationship that thrives is one where both individuals are willing to adapt to each other's needs. The way you communicate, support one another, and manage challenges cannot remain fixed in one season. To remain connected, you must adjust to new realities without losing love and respect.

Consider how friendships shift when people get married, move, or pursue different careers. What once worked— long hours spent together or constant communication— may no longer be realistic. Adaptability enables you to redefine the relationship while still nurturing its foundation. Instead of seeing the changes as a loss, you learn to embrace them as part of growth.

In family life, adaptability is just as crucial. Parents, for instance, must constantly adjust as children grow from infants to adults. What worked in one stage no longer fits in another. A parent who refuses to adapt risks creating distance, while one who embraces change fosters deeper trust and connection.

Healthy relationships are built on both stability and flexibility. Core values like respect, honesty, and love remain unchanged, but the ways we express them must evolve. Adaptability ensures that relationships are not rigid structures that break under pressure but living bonds that grow stronger through change.

Adaptability in Work and Over Careers

Few areas of life reveal the necessity of adaptability more clearly than the workplace. Technology shifts rapidly, industries rise and fall, and job requirements evolve year by year. Those who resist learning new skills often find themselves left behind, while adaptable individuals remain relevant and valuable. Adaptability is no longer optional in a career—it is essential.

The workplace often presents unexpected changes, such as restructuring, new leadership, or sudden changes in demand. These shifts can feel overwhelming, but they also provide opportunities to demonstrate resilience and creativity. By adjusting quickly, employees demonstrate their ability to thrive in uncertainty and often open doors to advancement.

Adaptability also requires letting go of the mindset that success follows a straight path. Careers rarely unfold in neat, predictable steps. Instead, they often involve detours, unexpected turns, and opportunities disguised as challenges. Those who adapt with grace and determination frequently discover paths to success they never imagined.

The key is to remain a learner in every season. Whether by mastering new technologies, developing interpersonal skills, or learning to lead in different contexts, adaptable people position themselves for long-term success. They are not shaken by change but empowered by it, knowing it is often the birthplace of innovation and growth.

Balancing Flexibility and Core Values

True adaptability requires balance. Flexibility does not mean abandoning the principles that guide your life. In fact, adaptability becomes dangerous when it compromises core values. The challenge is learning to adjust methods while staying grounded in the unchanging truths that define who you are.

Think of values as the roots of a tree and adaptability as its branches. The branches sway, bend, and move with the wind, but the roots remain firmly in the ground. In the same way, you can change your strategies, shift your routines, and adapt to new realities while remaining anchored in your deepest convictions.

Losing sight of core values in the name of change leads to instability. People who adapt by abandoning principles often lose their sense of identity. They may gain temporary success, but at the cost of integrity and peace. Adaptability only has value when it strengthens who you are, not when it erases it.

By balancing flexibility with faithfulness to your values, you create a powerful combination. You are steady in what matters most, yet agile enough to adjust to the demands of life. This balance creates a sense of peace even in uncertain times, allowing you to thrive no matter what changes come your way.

The Gift of a Teachable Spirit

At the heart of adaptability is a teachable spirit. A person who believes they already know everything tends to resist change and closes themselves off from growth. But one who is humble enough to learn remains open to correction, wisdom, and new perspectives. Teachability is the fuel that keeps adaptability alive.

Being teachable requires humility because it acknowledges that there is always more to learn. This humility prevents pride from making us rigid or unwilling to listen. A teachable person does not view correction as an attack but as an opportunity to grow. In this way, they continue to improve even in difficult seasons.

Teachability also makes us approachable. People are drawn to those who are willing to listen and learn rather than those who believe they have all the answers. This openness often leads to deeper relationships and greater opportunities in both personal and professional life.

A teachable spirit keeps us fresh, relevant, and ready for the future. Life will always introduce new challenges, but those who remain teachable can adjust, evolve, and thrive. Adaptability without teachability is impossible, but together they create a powerful foundation for lasting success.

Embracing Change, Thriving in Life

Adaptability is not simply a skill to master—it is a way of life that opens the door to growth in every season. When you choose to see change as an opportunity, stay curious in learning, and bounce back with resilience, you step into a life of strength and confidence. The storms of life may shake you, but they will not break you, because you have built the ability to bend and rise again. This mindset transforms what others see as threats into stepping stones for your next level of success.

In relationships, adaptability enables love and connection to mature instead of wither. In your career, it positions you to stay ahead while others remain stuck in outdated ways. In personal growth, it ensures that you never stop learning, never stop evolving, and never stop becoming the person you are meant to be. Every area of life becomes richer when you embrace the truth that flexibility is a strength, not a weakness.

The greatest danger of resisting change is missing the opportunities it brings. Life will not wait for you to feel ready—it moves forward whether you adapt or not. But the moment you decide to adjust, to learn, and to move with the shifts around you, you take control of your destiny. Change may be uncomfortable, but it is often the very tool God uses to grow your character and prepare you for blessings ahead.

Remember, adaptability does not mean abandoning your values or losing sight of who you are. Instead, it means carrying your principles with you into new seasons and applying them in fresh ways. Your values keep you rooted, while your adaptability helps you stretch toward the light of new opportunities. Together, they create a balance that gives you both strength and flexibility for the journey ahead.

As you step into a changing world, embrace adaptability as your ally. Don't fear the unknown—welcome it with faith, courage, and readiness to grow. Each shift you encounter is a chance to refine your character, strengthen your purpose, and expand your horizons. The world will keep moving, but with adaptability, you won't just keep up—you will thrive.

CHAPTER 4

PRINCIPLE 4: EMOTIONAL INTELLIGENCE – MASTERING YOURSELF AND YOUR RELATIONSHIPS

"A person without self-control is like a city with broken-down walls."
—Proverbs 25:28 (NLT)

The Hidden Key to Success

Walls in ancient times were more than barriers of stone—they were symbols of strength, security, and protection. A city without walls was vulnerable, exposed to attacks, and unable to withstand the pressures of the outside world. In the same way, a person without self-control is left unguarded, at the mercy of every emotion, every impulse, and every conflict that arises. Emotional intelligence begins with this truth: mastering yourself is the first line of defense against the chaos of life.

Success in life is often measured by achievements, titles, or financial milestones, but there is another force that quietly shapes every meaningful outcome: emotional intelligence. Emotional intelligence is the ability to recognize, understand, and manage your own emotions while also being able to understand and influence the emotions of others. Without it, intelligence alone can make you rigid, and talent alone can make you prideful. Emotional intelligence balances knowledge with compassion, ambition with humility, and achievement with influence.

In a rapidly changing world, emotional intelligence is the foundation of healthy relationships, effective leadership, and long-term happiness. A person may climb quickly through skills and talent, but without emotional maturity, their success often collapses under the weight of conflict or pride. The truth is that people rarely remember what you did for them, but they always remember how you made them feel. That is why mastering yourself and your relationships is essential for a fulfilling life.

Emotional intelligence is not just about being "nice" or avoiding conflict. It requires courage, self-awareness, and intentional growth. It involves setting boundaries, listening deeply, and responding with wisdom rather than impulse. This principle, when applied consistently, can change not only the way you live but also the way others experience you.

Let us now explore how emotional intelligence works in practice: how it begins with self-awareness, expands into self-control, strengthens through empathy, is lived out in effective communication, deepens through consistency in relationships, extends into financial discipline, and ultimately reveals itself in the reward of faithful living. By cultivating this principle, you are not only preparing yourself for success but ensuring that your success is sustainable, impactful, and rooted in character.

The Foundation of Self-Awareness

Self-awareness is the starting point of emotional intelligence. It means having a clear understanding of your emotions, strengths, weaknesses, values, and motivations. Too often, people live on autopilot, unaware of how their emotions drive their decisions and shape their relationships. Without self-awareness, frustration can turn into anger, ambition into arrogance, and stress into burnout. Recognizing what you feel and why you feel it gives you the power to direct your responses rather than being controlled by them.

Developing self-awareness requires slowing down and practicing honest reflection. When you notice frustration rising, ask yourself, *Why am I feeling this way? What does this emotion reveal about my expectations or fears?* This pause allows you to respond thoughtfully instead of reacting impulsively. Over time, self-awareness creates clarity. You notice patterns in your behavior—what triggers you, what motivates you, and what drains you. With that knowledge, you gain the ability to steer your life with greater purpose and direction.

Self-awareness also allows you to align your actions with your core values. For example, if integrity is important to you, being aware of moments where you're tempted to compromise helps you make choices that honor your principles. This alignment creates inner peace because you're living authentically. On the other hand, ignoring self-awareness often leads to inner conflict, regret, and broken trust.

A powerful truth about self-awareness is that it does not weaken you—it strengthens you. It takes humility to admit areas of weakness, but that humility opens the door to growth. It also makes you more approachable to others because people respect leaders and friends who are real, not perfect. Self-awareness lays the groundwork for all other dimensions of emotional intelligence. Without it, growth in different areas becomes shallow and unsustainable.

The Power of Self-Control

Once you become aware of your emotions, the next challenge is learning to manage them. Self-control does not mean ignoring or suppressing feelings, but instead directing them in ways that lead to constructive outcomes. Imagine being in a heated conversation at work where someone challenges your decision. Without self-control, you might snap back defensively, leaving a tension that lingers for weeks. With self-control, you pause, breathe, and choose to respond with clarity rather than emotion. That choice builds respect and influence.

One example comes from a man who worked in a fast-paced warehouse. Every day, he faced associates who arrived late, broke small rules, or made careless mistakes. At first, his instinct was to correct them harshly on the spot. But he noticed morale dropping and errors increasing. When he shifted his approach—pausing to ask questions, listening to the reasons, and correcting with firmness but calmness—he found the team responded better. His self-control not only improved their performance but also won him their trust.

Self-control also applies to personal habits. Consider a person who wants to save money but spends impulsively whenever stress hits. By practicing self-control—choosing to pause before buying, setting small rules for spending, or delaying gratification—they slowly change their financial trajectory. The discipline of self-control in the moment builds long-term freedom. What once felt restrictive eventually becomes empowering.

There will always be moments when emotions try to override wisdom. Stress, anger, excitement, and even joy can push us into decisions we later regret. But self-control is like the steering wheel of your life: without it, even a powerful car goes off course; with it, you can direct your path, no matter how intense the emotions or difficult the circumstances. This discipline transforms emotional intelligence into visible results.

Empathy: Stepping Into Another's Shoes

Empathy is the ability to understand and share others' feelings. It is what makes relationships thrive and what turns leaders into people others want to follow. A young woman once shared how she struggled at her job because her manager only cared about numbers. He never asked about her workload or listened to her challenges. Eventually, she quit, not because of the job itself, but because she felt invisible. That experience is a reminder that people will endure challenging work if they feel seen, but they will leave if they feel ignored.

To practice empathy, you must slow down and listen. Many people listen only to reply, but genuine empathy listens to understand. For instance, if a friend says, "I'm tired of everything," the empathetic response isn't to quickly offer solutions. It's to lean in and ask, "What's been weighing on you?" That kind of presence tells the other person, "You matter." Even when you cannot fix the problem, empathy heals by acknowledging the pain.

In family life, empathy strengthens bonds. A father who takes the time to understand why his teenage son is distant may learn that it's not rebellion, but the weight of peer pressure and insecurity. By listening and reassuring instead of punishing, he builds trust and connection. Similarly, marriages built on empathy weather storms better because both partners feel safe to express themselves without fear of judgment.

Empathy also carries power in leadership. Leaders who understand their people's struggles can inspire deeper loyalty. For example, a supervisor who notices an associate struggling physically and rearranges tasks for them communicates care. That act, though small, multiplies in impact because it makes others feel valued. Empathy is not weakness—it is strength expressed in kindness.

Communication: The Bridge of Understanding

Communication is where emotional intelligence is tested most. You may feel deeply and empathize sincerely, but if you cannot communicate effectively, relationships suffer. Good communication is not just about speaking clearly—it is about choosing words that build, tone that calms, and timing that respects. Many conflicts arise not from the issue itself, but from how it was communicated.

Consider two coworkers assigned to the same project. One was frustrated because the other seemed careless. Instead of exploding, she scheduled a private conversation and explained how the mistakes affected the team's deadlines. To her surprise, the coworker admitted he didn't understand parts of the task and was embarrassed to ask for clarification. By opening dialogue with respect, she transformed frustration into teamwork. That is the power of intentional communication.

At home, communication shapes the environment of love and trust. A spouse who only criticizes will crush confidence, while one who balances correction with affirmation creates an atmosphere of growth. Parents who take the time to explain rules rather than bark orders raise children who understand, not just obey. Communication builds either walls or bridges, depending on how it is used.

Effective communication also requires listening as much as speaking. Too often, people prepare their defense while the other person is still talking. But emotional intelligence demands full attention, listening for meaning, tone, and emotion. When others feel heard, they naturally become more open to hearing you. Communication, therefore, becomes a cycle of trust rather than a battlefield of words.

Consistency in Relationships

As we saw in chapter two, relationships thrive not on grand gestures but on steady, consistent actions. A friend who checks in regularly is more reliable than one who shows up only in moments of crisis. Emotional intelligence teaches us that consistency builds trust, while unpredictability creates anxiety. For example, a mother who consistently encourages her child builds a sense of safety. The child learns that love is steady, not conditional.

One example comes from a workplace where two managers were compared. One was brilliant but inconsistent, sometimes supportive, other times harsh without reason. The other manager was steady, always treating people with respect, even during stressful times. The second manager earned greater loyalty, not because she was the smartest, but because her team always knew what to expect from her. Consistency becomes a silent anchor in both personal and professional relationships.

Friendships are strengthened the same way. Think about the friend who always remembers your birthday, who shows up when you are sick, who checks in when you've been quiet. These small, steady acts build a bond stronger than occasional big favors. Emotional intelligence helps you see that it is not the size of the act that matters most, but the steadiness of your presence.

Consistency also helps in resolving conflict. When someone knows you will respond calmly and reasonably, they feel safer opening up. In contrast, if your reactions swing wildly, people will hide their struggles and fears from you. By practicing consistency, you not only make others feel secure but also make your relationships more resilient in the face of life's challenges.

Discipline in Finances

Emotional intelligence does not stop at relationships—it extends into how you manage your resources, including money. Many financial struggles stem not from a lack of income, but from a lack of emotional control. Overspending often springs from stress, envy, or the desire for comfort. By learning to regulate emotions, you can make wiser financial choices. For instance, resisting the urge to buy unnecessary items today creates room for savings that provide stability tomorrow.

Consider a young couple just starting out. They dreamed of buying a home but found themselves constantly short of savings. After reflecting, they realized much of their spending was driven by emotion—buying gadgets to keep up with peers, eating out to relieve stress, and shopping impulsively. Once they practiced discipline—choosing to cook at home, save before spending, and delay gratification—they began to see progress. Their emotional intelligence helped them distinguish between needs and wants, and soon they achieved their goal.

As we touched on in chapter two, financial discipline is also about consistency. It's not just about saving for one month, but about creating habits that last for years. Small acts, like setting aside a portion of each paycheck, compound into significant results over time. Emotional intelligence helps here by reducing the temptation to compare yourself to others. Instead, you focus on your own goals and build confidence through steady progress.

The truth is that financial stability is less about numbers and more about mindset. When you control your emotions, you stop letting money control you. You can say no to instant pleasure because you are focused on long-term peace. That discipline creates not just wealth but also the freedom to make choices that align with your values.

The Reward of Faithful Living

At the heart of emotional intelligence is faithful living—choosing to act with integrity, patience, and consistency over time. Faithfulness is often overlooked in a world that celebrates quick wins and overnight success. But those who remain faithful—to their values, their commitments, and their relationships—build lives of lasting impact. Emotional intelligence is the engine that allows faithfulness to thrive because it steadies your emotions through highs and lows.

There is a story of a man who worked at the same company for decades. He was not the loudest or the most talented, but he was faithful. He showed up on time, treated people with respect, and did his work with care. Over the years, his steady presence became a source of stability for others. When he retired, dozens of people testified to how his faithful life had shaped theirs. His legacy was not in titles but in the impact of his consistency.

Faithful living also applies in family life. A spouse who consistently shows love, even in small ways, builds a marriage that lasts. A parent who steadily models patience and integrity gives their children a blueprint for adulthood. These daily choices of faithfulness may seem ordinary, but they create extraordinary results over time.

Emotional intelligence makes faithful living possible because it helps you navigate frustration, disappointment, and temptation without giving up. It reminds you that consistency is more powerful than bursts of effort. The reward of faithful living is peace of mind, deeper relationships, and the quiet satisfaction of knowing you stayed true to who you are.

The Strength of Emotional Intelligence

Emotional intelligence is not an accessory to success—it is the foundation. It teaches you to know yourself, master your emotions, connect with others, and live faithfully. Without it, talent collapses under pressure, relationships crumble in conflict, and success feels empty. With it, you build a life that is steady, meaningful, and inspiring to others.

The true strength of emotional intelligence lies in its ripple effect. When you practice self-awareness, you inspire honesty. When you show empathy, you inspire kindness. When you remain consistent, you inspire trust. Emotional intelligence multiplies impact because it spreads through the lives you touch.

Life will always bring challenges, but emotional intelligence equips you to face them with wisdom, patience, and grace. Instead of reacting in anger, you respond with calm. Instead of breaking under stress, you adapt with resilience. Instead of chasing empty success, you build success that endures.

As you grow in this principle, remember that your greatest achievements will not be measured only by what you did, but by how you made people feel along the way. Mastering yourself and your relationships is one of the highest forms of success, and it is a gift you can give to every person you encounter.

CHAPTER 5

PRINCIPLE 5: GROWTH MINDSET – BECOMING A LIFELONG LEARNER

"Wise people are always learning, always listening for fresh insights." —Proverbs 18:15 (MSG)

The Power of How You Think

Your mindset is the lens through which you see the world. Two people can face the same challenge—one sees it as a dead end, the other sees it as an opportunity to grow. The difference is not in the challenge but in the mindset. A fixed mindset says, *This is all I am, and this is all I'll ever be.* A growth mindset declares, *I can learn, I can improve, and I can get stronger through this.*

Happiness and fulfillment are not found in flawless performance or perfect circumstances but in the joy of progress. A growth mindset turns setbacks into lessons and failures into stepping stones. It allows you to see yourself not as a finished product but as a work in progress, constantly improving. This way of thinking is what keeps people from becoming stuck in the past or imprisoned by limitations.

A fixed mindset, on the other hand, creates walls that keep you trapped. It whispers lies like, *I'm not smart enough, I wasn't born talented,* or *It's too late for me.* These beliefs paralyze potential and rob people of growth. But the truth is that anyone can change, learn, and grow if they are willing to shift how they see themselves. A growth mindset is the bridge to freedom.

Throughout this chapter, we will explore what it truly means to develop a growth mindset by contrasting the fixed mindset with the growth mindset, embracing challenges as opportunities, learning through failure, staying curious and hungry, applying a growth mindset in relationships, and discovering the joy of lifelong learning. Along the way, we will see how this principle not only transforms careers but also strengthens relationships, builds resilience, and creates lasting joy.

As we journey through these sections, let this principle challenge you to see yourself differently. Your story is not finished, and your future is not fixed. Every challenge is an invitation to grow. Every failure is a lesson waiting to be learned. Every relationship is an opportunity to strengthen your perspective. And every day brings a new chance to expand your knowledge and your capacity for joy. This is the power of a growth mindset: it equips you not just to survive, but to thrive in life.

Fixed Mindset vs. Growth Mindset

To understand the growth mindset, we must first recognize its opposite. A fixed mindset is rooted in the belief that your abilities and intelligence are set in stone. People with this mindset often avoid challenges because they fear failure will expose their limitations. Instead of stretching themselves, they stay in their comfort zones, where things feel safe but stagnant. Over time, this leads to frustration, lack of progress, and even bitterness.

Consider a student who struggles in math. With a fixed mindset, they might think, *I'm just not good at numbers, and stop trying.* Every test becomes a confirmation of their limitation. But with a growth mindset, that same student would say, "I'm not good at this yet, but with practice I can improve." The word *yet* becomes a powerful bridge from failure to growth. That mindset shifts effort from wasted energy into an investment.

We see the same difference in the workplace. One employee may avoid new projects because they fear making mistakes. Another eagerly volunteers, knowing mistakes will teach them valuable lessons. Over time, the second employee grows in skills and confidence, while the first remains stagnant. The difference is not talent—it is mindset.

A growth mindset does not deny the existence of difficulty. Instead, it embraces challenges as opportunities to stretch and grow. This perspective transforms obstacles into stepping stones. By recognizing where we've fallen into fixed thinking, we open the door to growth that leads to both success and fulfillment.

Embracing Challenges as Opportunities

Every person encounters challenges, but the difference between those who stagnate and those who thrive lies in how they interpret those challenges. For someone with a fixed mindset, obstacles appear as walls—signals that they should stop trying or that they have reached their limit. In contrast, those with a growth mindset see obstacles as doors waiting to be opened. They ask themselves, *What can I learn here? How can this situation make me stronger?* This shift transforms what seems like a setback into a stepping stone toward growth.

Consider a young athlete who trained for years to qualify for a major competition. When they failed to make the cut on their first attempt, they could have given up, concluding that they "just weren't good enough." Instead, they studied their performance, identified weaknesses, and adjusted their training. On their second attempt, they not only qualified but exceeded their previous scores. The initial failure became the exact challenge that built the discipline and strength they needed to succeed.

In the workplace, this principle applies just as powerfully. An employee might be assigned a project far outside their comfort zone. At first, the task feels overwhelming, and the temptation to quit arises. But rather than walking away, the growth-minded person leans in, researches what they don't know, and asks for help from mentors or colleagues. By the end, they emerge not only with a completed project but also with new skills and greater confidence. The challenge became a hidden opportunity for advancement.

Even in personal life, challenges can serve as opportunities if approached with the right mindset. A difficult relationship, for example, may reveal areas where one needs to grow in patience, communication, or empathy. What seems like a burden at first can, with reflection and effort, strengthen character and emotional intelligence. The struggle itself becomes the classroom in which wisdom is earned.

When you embrace challenges as opportunities, you stop fearing them and begin welcoming them as essential parts of your journey. Each challenge you face shapes you into someone stronger, wiser, and more prepared for the next step. Instead of being intimidated by difficulty, you come to see it as a signal that growth is on the horizon.

Learning Through Failure

Failure is one of life's greatest teachers, though most people do everything in their power to avoid it. A fixed mindset interprets failure as proof of inadequacy: *I wasn't good enough, or I'll never get it right*. However, a growth mindset views failure differently: it is not the end of the journey, but a critical part of the process. Each failure carries with it a lesson that equips you for greater success, and without failure, there is no feedback, no correction, no actual progress.

Think about a child learning to walk. They stumble, fall, and cry. Yet, no parent interprets these falls as failure— they see them as part of the process of walking. Each fall strengthens the child's balance and teaches them how to adjust their steps. In the same way, every time we fall in life, we are being trained to walk more steadily into our purpose. The key is to keep getting up after every fall.

Take, for instance, a small business owner who launches their first shop only to see it close within the first year. To some, this looks like a disaster. But the entrepreneur with a growth mindset treats it as a classroom. They study where they miscalculated—perhaps they didn't manage their cash flow well, or they overlooked marketing. With these lessons in hand, they try again, this time stronger, wiser, and more prepared. The so-called "failure" becomes the very soil from which future success grows.

Failure also builds resilience. Each time you fall and rise again, you prove to yourself that setbacks are not final. This resilience is what allows you to face even bigger challenges down the road with courage. Without the sting of past failures, you would never develop the grit necessary to persevere when the stakes are higher. In this sense, failure is not a roadblock but a conditioning exercise, preparing you for the weight of future responsibilities.

Finally, learning through failure reminds us to be humble. It teaches us that we don't know everything, and that wisdom often comes at a cost. But that cost pays dividends in the long run. Those who refuse to learn from failure remain stuck, but those who embrace it gain wisdom, strength, and vision. With the proper perspective, failure is not a dead end but a detour that leads you exactly where you need to be.

Staying Curious and Hungry

Curiosity is the fuel of growth. When you maintain a hunger to learn, you open doors that would otherwise remain shut. A fixed mindset says, *I already know enough,* but a growth mindset asks, *What else can I discover?* This posture keeps you humble, eager, and ready to embrace growth opportunities. Without curiosity, people become stagnant; with it, they remain alive, adaptable, and forward-moving.

Consider someone who has worked in the same job for years. They could easily settle into routine and assume there's nothing new to learn. But the growth-minded person remains curious, asking themselves questions like: *What new skill could help me in my role? How is technology changing my field? What habits can I adopt to be more effective?* This hunger for learning not only enhances their performance but also makes them invaluable to their team. The difference is not talent—it's curiosity and persistence.

Curiosity also protects against complacency. Many people achieve a small measure of success and then stop pushing forward, thinking they have "arrived." But the truth is, success is never final—it requires continued learning and adjustment. A curious person treats success as a foundation, not a finish line. They remain hungry for growth, constantly exploring new ideas, strategies, and perspectives. That hunger keeps their success alive and growing, rather than fading over time.

On a personal level, curiosity enriches life itself. A person who stays hungry for knowledge and experience lives with a sense of wonder. They read new books, try new activities, and explore unfamiliar places. This mindset makes life more exciting and full. Even simple things—a conversation with someone from another culture, learning a new recipe, or developing a new hobby— become opportunities for growth. This joy of discovery adds depth and meaning to everyday life.

Spiritually, curiosity and hunger remind us that there is always more to learn and more ways to grow in character.

The humble person knows they haven't "arrived" and that each day offers lessons for patience, wisdom, or compassion. This hunger for growth doesn't just make us smarter—it makes us better people. It pushes us beyond comfort zones and teaches us to embrace life as an ongoing journey of becoming.

A Growth Mindset in Relationships

Relationships are one of the clearest areas where a growth mindset makes a difference. Too often, people enter friendships, marriages, or family connections with the idea that people are "just the way they are" and cannot change. This fixed mindset creates frustration, distance, and even brokenness. But when we apply a growth mindset to relationships, we begin to see people—including ourselves—as works in progress. We learn to be patient with flaws, celebrate small improvements, and believe in the possibility of growth.

Think of two friends who disagree often. A fixed mindset says, That's just how he is—we'll never get along. A growth mindset responds differently: We may not see eye to eye, but we can learn from each other and grow stronger through this. This latter perspective transforms conflict into an opportunity for deeper understanding, rather than a wall that divides. It allows forgiveness, grace, and reconciliation to thrive because growth-minded people don't expect perfection—they expect progress.

In marriage, a growth mindset is essential. Every couple faces challenges, whether it's financial stress, parenting struggles, or differences in communication. A fixed mindset leads couples to believe they're incompatible or doomed to fail. But a growth mindset says, *We can learn how to navigate this together.* This doesn't mean every problem vanishes, but it does mean both partners commit to learning, adjusting, and improving together. Over time, this attitude deepens trust and strengthens the bond, creating a partnership built on resilience.

Friendships and family relationships also benefit when we embrace the growth mindset. Instead of holding people hostage to their past mistakes, we give them room to change and grow. We also hold ourselves accountable to become better friends, siblings, or parents. For example, someone who grew up in a home where affection wasn't shown may struggle to express love. With a growth mindset, they can unlearn old patterns and intentionally develop new, healthier habits. This willingness to grow transforms not just individuals but entire family legacies.

At its core, a growth mindset in relationships is about hope. It believes that people are not locked into their worst moments but can rise above them. It encourages grace, patience, and encouragement rather than judgment or despair. When applied consistently, this mindset creates environments where love, trust, and understanding flourish. Relationships become less about demanding perfection and more about journeying together toward growth.

The Joy of Lifelong Learning

Lifelong learning is more than acquiring knowledge—it is a mindset that transforms every experience into an opportunity for growth. People with a growth mindset approach life as an endless classroom, seeking lessons in both success and failure. They understand that learning does not stop when formal education ends—it continues every day through observation, reflection, and practice. This perspective turns ordinary moments into chances for improvement, making life richer, fuller, and more meaningful.

Consider a mid-career professional who feels stagnant in their role. Rather than resigning to boredom, they choose to study new skills, attend workshops, and seek feedback from colleagues. Over time, this dedication to learning rejuvenates their career and opens opportunities that would have otherwise been missed. The joy comes not just from advancement, but also from the sense of growth and mastery that accompanies each new skill. Every small victory becomes a celebration of progress, fueling continued effort.

Lifelong learning also encourages curiosity in daily life. It might be exploring a new hobby, reading widely outside our field, or engaging with people who challenge our thinking. A person who embraces lifelong learning remains agile and adaptable, even in times of uncertainty. For example, someone who learns about digital tools or emerging technologies can navigate shifts in their industry with confidence, while those who resist change may struggle. Learning keeps the mind sharp, the spirit motivated, and the heart engaged.

This principle extends beyond career or personal hobbies—it applies to character and relationships as well. Lifelong learners actively seek to understand themselves, recognize areas for emotional growth, and improve communication skills. A parent might read about child development to better support their child's growth, or a partner might learn new ways to express love and empathy. The joy of lifelong learning is that it enhances every facet of life, from work to relationships to personal fulfillment.

Finally, lifelong learning is intrinsically tied to humility. The more you learn, the more you realize how much you do not know. This awareness fosters openness, gratitude, and a desire to keep improving. When you see every challenge as a lesson and every interaction as an opportunity to grow, life becomes a dynamic journey rather than a static routine. Lifelong learning is not a task—it is a mindset that brings continuous joy and empowerment.

Keep Growing, Keep Thriving

Embracing a growth mindset is not a one-time decision—
it is a lifelong commitment to becoming the best version
of yourself. Every challenge you face, every failure you
encounter, and every new skill you learn is part of a journey
toward greater wisdom, resilience, and fulfillment. By
seeing challenges as opportunities, learning from failure,
staying curious, and nurturing your relationships, you
create a life that is dynamic, meaningful, and impactful.

The world will continue to change, and circumstances
will often push you outside your comfort zone. Those
with a growth mindset do not resist these shifts—they
lean into them. They understand that growth comes from
effort, reflection, and the courage to try again. Like a
tree whose roots deepen through storms, your character
and abilities strengthen with every trial you face. The joy
is not only in the achievements but in the transformation
that occurs along the way.

Lifelong learning is at the heart of this principle. When
you commit to learning continually about your field,
yourself, and the people around you, you remain adaptable,
innovative, and inspired. Curiosity fuels progress, and
each step forward, no matter how small, compounds into
extraordinary results over time. Your journey becomes
not just about what you achieve but about who you are
becoming through each experience.

Remember, happiness is found in progress, not perfection. By cultivating a growth mindset, you give yourself the freedom to fail, the courage to persevere, and the perspective to appreciate every lesson life offers. You transform obstacles into opportunities, stagnation into momentum, and fear into confidence. Your life becomes a living testament to the power of resilience, learning, and continuous growth.

So, take the lessons of this chapter to heart: face challenges with courage, learn from every setback, remain hungry for knowledge, nurture your relationships, and embrace the endless journey of growth. Your potential is not fixed, your abilities are not limited, and your story is far from finished. The life you desire—one of achievement, joy, and lasting fulfillment—is waiting for you, step by step, lesson by lesson, growth by growth.

CHAPTER 6

PRINCIPLE 6: BALANCE AND WELL-BEING – SUCCESS WITHOUT BURNOUT

"Better one handful with tranquility than two handfuls with toil and chasing after the wind."—Ecclesiastes 4:6

Balance and Well-Being – Success Without Burnout

What good is success if it comes at the expense of your health, peace, or relationships? Too many people chase achievements at the cost of the very things that give life meaning. They work tirelessly, sacrificing sleep, health, and time with loved ones, only to discover later that the prize they pursued left them empty and exhausted. True happiness is not found in the constant grind, but in the ability to balance ambition with gratitude, striving with enjoying, and work with rest. Success, without balance, is fragile and unsustainable.

Balance is not about doing less or lowering your standards. It is about aligning your priorities so that every area of your life supports, rather than competes with, the others. Just as a symphony requires each instrument to play in harmony, life requires us to keep work, health, relationships, and faith in alignment. If even one area is ignored, the harmony turns into noise. Balance is the art of living with intention, creating a rhythm that allows us to grow while remaining grounded.

In this chapter, we will explore the principle of balance through several key areas: the rhythm of work and rest, health as wealth, guarding your peace through emotional and spiritual well-being, the power of rest and renewal, relationships as the heart of true success, and gratitude and contentment as the secret to lasting happiness. Each of these areas is not a luxury but a necessity for anyone who desires lasting success and genuine fulfillment.

Think of balance as the invisible thread that holds together all the other principles we have explored so far. Discipline, adaptability, emotional intelligence, and a growth mindset all gain their strength when practiced in balance. Without it, even the greatest discipline becomes drudgery, adaptability becomes instability, and emotional intelligence becomes exhaustion. With balance, however, these qualities can thrive and enrich not only your own life but also the lives of those around you.

This is the principle that protects you from burnout, anchors you during stress, and allows you to enjoy the fruits of your labor without losing yourself in the process. As we journey through this chapter, you will see how balance is not only possible but also deeply rewarding. It does not require perfection, but it does require intentional choices. Let's dive into what it looks like to build a life of balance and well-being.

The Rhythm of Work and Rest

One of the greatest lessons life offers is that work without rest leads to destruction. Just as our bodies need sleep to recover, our minds and spirits require moments of renewal. Many people confuse rest with laziness, but rest is not the absence of productivity—it is what makes productivity sustainable. Without it, burnout becomes inevitable.

Think of a farmer who works the land season after season without allowing it to rest. Eventually, the soil becomes depleted, and no amount of labor will bring forth a good harvest. The same principle applies to life. If you never pause, your energy, creativity, and joy will dry up. Rest is not wasted time—it is an investment in your ability to keep going with strength and clarity.

Rest also has many forms. It can be physical, such as through sleep or relaxation. It can be emotional, such as spending time with loved ones or enjoying hobbies. Or it can be spiritual, by setting aside time for prayer, reflection, and gratitude. Each form of rest replenishes a part of you that work alone cannot. Skipping rest might help you finish a short-term task, but embracing it ensures long-term success and fulfillment.

When you create a rhythm between work and rest, you step into a flow that energizes rather than exhausts. You no longer live in cycles of overwork followed by collapse. Instead, you find a sustainable pace that allows you to achieve much while still having the strength to enjoy the fruits of your labor. Balance here is not about doing less—it is about doing wisely.

Health as Wealth

There's an old saying that "a healthy person has a thousand dreams, but a sick person has only one." It's a reminder that no matter how much success we chase, without our health—physical, mental, and emotional—everything else fades into the background. Wealth loses its shine if you don't have the energy to enjoy it. Recognition feels hollow if you're too burned out to celebrate. Many ambitious people make the mistake of thinking their health is something they can sacrifice today and recover tomorrow. But the truth is, every late night, every skipped meal, every ignored doctor's appointment adds up. The body and mind keep score.

Consider James, a high-performing executive who climbed the corporate ladder at lightning speed. He prided himself on being the first one in the office and the last one to leave, surviving on caffeine and four hours of sleep. For years, he wore his exhaustion like a badge of honor. But one morning, at just forty-two years old, James collapsed at his desk from a heart scare. The wake-up call forced him to face a hard truth: he had built a successful career, but at the expense of the very thing that allowed him to enjoy it—his health. His story is not rare. Many people only realize the cost of neglect when the body finally demands payment.

Caring for your health is not selfish—it's strategic. Just as a car requires fuel and maintenance to run smoothly, your body needs rest, proper nutrition, and movement to perform at its best. Sleep is not wasted time—it's an investment in clarity, focus, and creativity. Exercise is not just about looking good—it's about keeping your energy tank full for the demands of leadership, family, and life. Even simple practices like walking, stretching, or drinking water consistently can become game-changers when they are prioritized.

Equally important is mental health. In our hyper-connected world, stress and anxiety are silent killers, robbing us of peace and clarity. The person who hustles without pause may achieve quick wins, but they risk long-term burnout. Practices like journaling, prayer, meditation, or simply unplugging from screens can restore balance to the mind. Protecting your mental health allows you to approach challenges with resilience instead of panic, with wisdom instead of weariness.

When you care for your health, you are multiplying your capacity for impact. A healthy leader inspires confidence. A healthy parent shows up fully for their children. A healthy friend contributes joy rather than draining energy. Health gives you margin, creativity, and longevity. In this sense, true wealth isn't just the money in your bank account but the strength in your body, the peace in your mind, and the joy in your spirit. Balance begins here, with the understanding that health is not a side benefit of success—it is success.

Guarding Your Peace: Emotional and Spiritual Well-Being

One of the greatest signs of wisdom is knowing what not to carry. In a world where noise, pressure, and expectations come from every direction, peace has become a rare treasure. You can succeed in business, earn the respect of others, and achieve financial freedom, but if your inner world is filled with chaos, it will all feel empty. Guarding your peace, emotionally and spiritually, is not about escaping life's challenges—it's about learning how to walk through them without being consumed.

Let us look at Anna, a successful entrepreneur who built her company from the ground up. On the outside, her life looked flawless: awards, recognition, and a team that admired her. But inside, she was restless. She allowed every email, every client complaint, and every dip in the market to steal her peace. It wasn't until she began practicing daily prayer and journaling, creating a sacred space to release her burdens, that she experienced true freedom. The business was still demanding, but she was no longer a prisoner to it. She learned that guarding her peace gave her the strength to lead with wisdom instead of fear.

Emotional well-being starts with boundaries. Not every battle is yours to fight, and not every opinion deserves your attention. People often think saying "yes" to everything is a sign of kindness, but in reality, it is a recipe for burnout. Learning to say "no" with grace is a form of self-respect and emotional protection. When you guard your time and energy, you create space to invest in what truly matters—your family, your growth, and your faith.

On the spiritual side, peace comes from connection to something greater than yourself. For many, this means faith in God, grounding them in values that don't shift with circumstances. For others, it may be practices of stillness, reflection, or gratitude. The point is that peace is not found in the absence of problems but in the presence of perspective. When your soul is anchored, storms may rage around you, but you remain steady.

Guarding your peace is a daily choice. It means being intentional about what you watch, what you listen to, and who you allow into your circle. It means unplugging from the constant noise of social media to recharge in silence. It means replacing fear-driven thoughts with affirmations of hope and truth. This emotional and spiritual balance doesn't just help you survive success—it ensures you can enjoy it without losing yourself along the way.

The Power of Rest and Renewal

In a culture that glorifies hustle, rest is often misunderstood as a sign of weakness. Yet history, science, and even faith traditions remind us that rest is not a luxury—it is a necessity. Without it, even the most talented, ambitious individuals eventually break down. Think of your body as a finely tuned machine. You can push it to perform at extraordinary levels, but without regular maintenance, it will wear out long before its time. Rest and renewal are the "maintenance" that allow us to sustain success without burning out.

Rest is not just physical—it is also mental. Our minds are constantly bombarded with information, from emails to news headlines to endless social media feeds. Without intentional breaks, mental exhaustion creeps in, leaving us unable to think clearly or make wise decisions. Something as simple as taking a walk in nature, meditating for ten minutes, or unplugging from screens in the evening can refresh the mind more than hours of "busy work." Renewal creates space for new ideas, fresh perspectives, and deeper insights.

Spiritually, rest has always been seen as sacred. It is in stillness that we reconnect with our values, our faith, and our purpose. Renewal allows us to remember that our worth is not measured by endless productivity, but by who we are becoming in the process. In those quiet pauses, we are often reminded of the bigger picture and why our work matters in the first place.

The power of rest and renewal is that it restores balance. It tells us that it is okay to pause, to breathe, to recover. Just as athletes schedule rest days to allow their muscles to grow stronger, we too must embrace periods of renewal to live stronger, healthier, and more fulfilled lives. Success gained at the expense of rest is temporary. Success built on consistent renewal, however, lasts a lifetime.

Relationships: The Heart of True Success

No matter how impressive your achievements may be, success feels empty if you have no one to share it with. Relationships are the anchor of a meaningful life. They provide love, support, and a sense of belonging that no career milestone or financial reward can replace. Many people discover this truth only after chasing accomplishments, only to find themselves alone when they finally arrive at the "top." True balance comes from nurturing the connections that give life depth and joy.

We can look at Maria, a successful entrepreneur who spent years building her company. Her business thrived, but her marriage and friendships slowly withered because she was "too busy." She often told herself she would make time for loved ones "later." When her health faltered and stress overwhelmed her, she realized her greatest wealth wasn't in her bank account but in the relationships she had neglected. By reordering her priorities—scheduling family dinners, calling friends regularly, and being present in conversations—she rediscovered a joy that no business success could provide.

Strong relationships require consistency, intentionality, and humility. It is not enough to give the people we love leftover energy after work or distractions. Just as we invest time and resources into our careers, we must also invest in the people who walk alongside us. A simple message of encouragement, a few minutes of undivided attention, or a habit of expressing gratitude can strengthen bonds more than grand gestures done infrequently. Balance means refusing to sacrifice your relationships on the altar of ambition.

Healthy relationships also serve as a mirror, reflecting who we truly are. A spouse, close friend, or family member can challenge us, hold us accountable, and encourage us to grow in ways we could never do alone. When we are balanced in our relationships, we gain both support in times of struggle and joy in times of celebration. These bonds remind us that life is not a solo journey but a shared one, meant to be lived together.

At the end of life, people rarely regret not working harder or earning more. Instead, they often regret the moments they missed with loved ones: the conversations unsaid, the milestones unattended, the love left unexpressed. Relationships are not a distraction from success—they are the essence of it. To live a life of balance and well-being is to remember that people matter more than profits, and love is a greater legacy than titles.

Gratitude and Contentment: The Secret to Lasting Happiness

In the pursuit of success, it is easy to believe that happiness will arrive when we achieve the next milestone—when we earn more money, gain recognition, or reach a certain position. Yet the truth is that happiness is not found in what we are chasing, but in what we already have. Gratitude is the practice of recognizing the blessings in front of us, and contentment is the peace that comes from knowing enough is already within our reach. Without gratitude, balance is impossible because the striving never ends.

James, a close friend of ours, always felt like he was one step behind in life. Every time he reached a goal, he quickly set another, never allowing himself to pause and celebrate. To outsiders, he appeared successful, but internally, he was restless and unsatisfied. His turning point came when a mentor challenged him to begin each day by writing down three things he was thankful for. At first, it felt forced, but over time, James noticed the small joys he had overlooked: a supportive spouse, his children's laughter, and his health. Gratitude shifted his focus from what was missing to what was already abundant, and with it came a sense of balance he had never known.

Gratitude does not mean we stop striving or abandon our goals. Instead, it anchors our ambition in joy rather than desperation. A grateful heart allows us to pursue dreams from a place of abundance, not lack. When we cultivate gratitude, work becomes less about proving ourselves and more about using our gifts. Contentment, likewise, is not laziness—it is the deep understanding that while growth is important, we do not need to compare ourselves to others to feel fulfilled constantly.

Gratitude also transforms relationships. When we express appreciation to others—whether through words, acts of kindness, or simply listening with full attention—we strengthen bonds and create an atmosphere of love. A spouse who feels appreciated, a friend who feels valued, or a colleague who feels acknowledged will respond with deeper trust and connection. In this way, gratitude not only enriches our personal happiness but also enriches the lives of those around us.

Contentment gives us the freedom to rest. Many people burn out not because they work hard, but because they never allow themselves to feel that they are "enough." Balance requires the humility to slow down, to say no to unnecessary pursuits, and to enjoy the blessings already present. Gratitude and contentment are the quiet forces that remind us that success without joy is not success at all. By practicing them daily, we ensure that our achievements are not only impressive but also deeply satisfying.

Living a Balanced and Fulfilled Life

Balance is not about doing everything at once—it is about doing what matters most with wisdom and intention. It is the steady rhythm between work and rest, ambition and gratitude, relationships, and personal growth. When we pursue success without balance, we risk losing the very things that make success meaningful: our health, our peace, and our loved ones. But when we embrace balance, we discover that actual achievement is not found in burnout but in a life that is whole, steady, and joyful.

Think back to the themes of this chapter: health, peace, relationships, and gratitude. Each one is like a pillar, holding up the foundation of a life well-lived. Without them, success collapses under the weight of exhaustion and emptiness. With them, success becomes sustainable and life-giving. Balance transforms achievement from a sprint that drains us into a journey that nourishes us.

Imagine building your life as a house. The walls represent discipline and focus, but the roof—the part that shields and completes everything—is balance. Without the roof, the house cannot protect you. Likewise, without balance, all other principles eventually crumble. To guard your health, protect your peace, and nurture your relationships is not weakness—it is strength. It is the wisdom of someone who knows that success should add to life, not strip it away.

The most inspiring lives are not those filled only with titles or wealth but those lived with joy, peace, and love. Picture yourself years from now, looking back not only on what you achieved but also on who you became in the process. Did you laugh with your family? Did you protect your body and mind? Did you build relationships that lasted? Did you live with gratitude? These are the questions balance allows you to answer with confidence and joy.

Thus, as you move forward, remember this: success without balance is a mirage, but success with balance is a legacy. Protect your health, guard your peace, rest often, love deeply, and live gratefully. By doing so, you will not only achieve your dreams but also enjoy them to the fullest. That is the kind of life worth striving for—a life of success without burnout, a life of balance and well-being.

CHAPTER 7

PRINCIPLE 7: RESILIENCE AND PERSEVERANCE - TURNING SETBACKS INTO SETUPS

"Not only so, but we also glory in our sufferings, because we know that suffering produces perseverance; perseverance, character; and character, hope."
—Romans 5:3–4

Life is rarely a straight path. Even the most determined, talented, and prepared individuals encounter obstacles, failures, and unexpected challenges. The difference between those who succeed and those who falter is not talent or luck—it is resilience. Resilience is the ability to rise again after setbacks, to view failure not as the end but as a stepping stone toward growth. It is perseverance in action, a refusal to let temporary defeat dictate your future.

Resilience begins with perspective. A setback can feel devastating in the moment, but it often contains lessons that become visible only when we reflect. Those who rise from challenges see the experience as an opportunity to learn, adapt, and grow stronger. Consider a small business owner whose store was destroyed in a fire. While many would have given up, they treated the disaster as a test of resourcefulness and community support, rebuilding not only the store but a more substantial customer base and a better business model. This ability to see opportunity in adversity is the hallmark of resilient individuals.

Perseverance is the companion to resilience. It is not enough to recover once—life demands repeated effort, day after day. Perseverance is cultivated through consistent action, even when motivation fades and progress seems slow. It is the small steps taken persistently that lead to the most significant victories. Stories of success are rarely about a single dramatic breakthrough—they are about continued effort, adjustment, and endurance over time.

Resilience is also deeply tied to emotional intelligence. The ability to manage emotions, remain calm under pressure, and respond thoughtfully rather than react impulsively is critical when facing setbacks. Those who master their emotions can clearly evaluate challenges, make sound decisions, and sustain hope even in difficult circumstances. Emotional balance, coupled with perseverance, transforms obstacles into opportunities for growth and development.

Another key aspect of resilience is mindset. Those who view setbacks as temporary and specific, rather than permanent and personal, are better equipped to bounce back. They replace "I failed" with "What can I learn?"

and "This is over" with "I can adjust and try again." This shift in thinking is not easy, but it is powerful. Each failure becomes a teacher, each obstacle a lesson, and each difficulty a chance to cultivate strength and character.

In the sections that follow, we will explore resilience in depth, examining how to understand setbacks as opportunities, cultivate perseverance through daily habits, learn to adapt emotionally, build mental toughness, strengthen character through challenges, and find hope and purpose amid trials. By the end of this chapter, you will see that resilience is not just surviving adversity—it is thriving because of it.

Understanding Setbacks as Setups

At first glance, setbacks often feel like detours that push us further from our goals. They can leave us questioning our abilities, doubting our decisions, and even wondering if success is meant for us at all. Yet many of the world's greatest breakthroughs were born not from smooth sailing but from hardship. Resilient people understand that every setback carries within it a seed of opportunity—sometimes hidden, sometimes painful, but always capable of producing growth if we choose to see it.

On a personal level, setbacks often refine us more than success ever could. When things come easily, we rarely stop to reflect, improve, or stretch ourselves. But when life knocks us down, we are forced to dig deeper, to reevaluate, and to discover strengths we never knew we had. A lost job can lead to a better career path. A failed relationship can teach us to love more wisely and more deeply. A financial struggle can cultivate habits of discipline and stewardship that success alone could never develop.

The key is how we interpret the moment. If we see a setback as a permanent failure, we surrender our power to rise. But if we view it as a temporary challenge, we unlock the ability to pivot, adapt, and move forward with new wisdom. This perspective doesn't make the pain disappear, but it gives it purpose. Pain with purpose is what transforms wounds into wisdom and stumbling blocks into stepping stones.

Spiritually, this principle is reinforced throughout scripture. In an Old Testament story, Joseph, betrayed by his brothers and sold into slavery, spent years in hardship before rising to become a leader in Egypt. What his brothers intended for harm, God used for good (Genesis 50:20). His setbacks positioned him to save a nation and reconcile with his family. The story of Joseph reminds us that sometimes what appears to be an ending is preparation for a greater calling.

Ultimately, setbacks are not stop signs—they are signposts pointing us toward growth. They ask us to pause, reflect, and realign our approach. Every delay, every disappointment, every detour has the potential to prepare us for the next stage of our journey. When we begin to see setbacks not as obstacles but as setups, we cultivate resilience that allows us to face the future with courage, hope, and determination.

Cultivating Perseverance Through Daily Habits

Perseverance is not built in the heat of crisis but in the rhythm of daily life. It is the product of small choices repeated consistently over time. Much like a musician mastering an instrument through hours of practice, we strengthen our ability to persevere by developing habits that anchor us when challenges come. These habits become our foundation, keeping us steady when life's storms threaten to knock us off our feet.

One of the most powerful habits is discipline in the small things: waking up early, finishing tasks with excellence, and keeping commitments. These may seem ordinary, but they develop a muscle of consistency that prepares us for greater battles. When setbacks occur, people who have cultivated daily discipline are less likely to succumb to discouragement because perseverance has become a part of their routine.

There were seasons in our own lives when balancing work and school felt almost impossible. After long shifts, the last thing we wanted to do was open a book, but we made it a habit to set aside at least an hour each night to study. Some nights, we were tired and tempted to quit, but we kept reminding ourselves of the futures we wanted to build. Looking back, the breakthroughs didn't come from one big moment of strength—it came from those small, steady choices that carried us through until graduation.

Daily habits also shape our perception of failure. Someone who journals daily, for example, learns to process emotions rather than bury them. A person who practices gratitude each morning trains their mind to see blessings even in the midst of hardship. These seemingly small disciplines rewire the way we think, helping us to persevere not with bitterness but with resilience and perspective.

Spiritual habits matter just as much. Prayer, meditation, and reflection on scripture build an inner strength that no external storm can easily break. These practices remind us of a bigger picture—that our lives have purpose beyond the momentary struggle. When we anchor our daily routines in both practical and spiritual habits, perseverance becomes less about willpower and more about being rooted in something greater than ourselves.

Ultimately, perseverance is not about avoiding exhaustion or pretending struggles don't exist. It is about building habits that sustain us when life feels overwhelming. These daily choices may not seem dramatic, but they build the strength to keep moving forward when everything within us wants to quit. Habits are the silent architects of perseverance, shaping the kind of people we become when the pressure is on.

Learning to Adapt Emotionally

Resilience is not only about physical endurance or the ability to work hard—it is also about emotional adaptability. Life rarely goes according to plan. Relationships can shift, opportunities may fall through, and circumstances can change in an instant. People who thrive are not those who avoid disappointment, but those who learn to adjust emotionally without letting bitterness or despair take root. Emotional adaptability allows us to bend without breaking.

For example, consider someone who loses a long-awaited job promotion. The first wave of disappointment is natural—it stings deeply. But what matters most is how they process that setback. Some might spiral into resentment, seeing themselves as a failure. Others might use the moment to reframe their perspective: *This role wasn't the right fit for me right now, but I can grow in the meantime and prepare for what's next.* This emotional pivot is what separates those who remain stuck from those who eventually rise stronger.

Adapting emotionally also means learning to let go of what we cannot control. Many people exhaust themselves emotionally by replaying "what could have been." Resilient individuals recognize the futility of this cycle. Instead, they focus their energy on what can be shaped and changed. A student who fails a major exam, for example, may feel crushed in the moment, but resilience comes when they choose to learn from the mistakes, adjust their study habits, and retake the test with renewed determination.

Another key to emotional adaptability is finding healthy outlets for processing pain. Bottling up emotions can create an inner weight that makes it difficult to move forward. Journaling, prayer, trusted conversations, or even physical exercise can help release the tension that setbacks create. By processing rather than suppressing, we give ourselves space to heal and recover. This doesn't erase the difficulty, but it allows us to carry it without being consumed by it.

Finally, adapting emotionally requires hope. Without hope, perseverance loses its fire. Hope reminds us that today's disappointment is not the end of our story. It pushes us to imagine a tomorrow where growth and redemption are not only possible but also attainable. Just as storms do not last forever, seasons of pain and setback eventually give way to new beginnings. When we adapt emotionally with hope, we shield our hearts from despair and remain open to the opportunities that lie ahead.

Building Mental Toughness

Mental toughness is the quiet strength that enables us to keep moving forward when everything around us says to stop. It is not about being emotionless or pretending difficulties don't hurt—it's about developing a mindset that chooses endurance over surrender. Just as an athlete conditions their body for competition, resilience requires conditioning the mind to face adversity with determination. Mental toughness doesn't eliminate hardship—it equips us to handle it without losing focus or hope.

One way to build mental toughness is by setting small but intentional challenges for ourselves. Each time we complete a task that stretches us beyond our comfort zone, we train our minds to persist through discomfort. For instance, a student who chooses to push through a complex subject rather than avoiding it develops not just knowledge, but grit. A worker who takes on a project outside their comfort zone learns to face uncertainty without being paralyzed by fear. Over time, these small victories accumulate into unshakable confidence that can withstand bigger trials.

Another key to mental toughness is learning to manage negative self-talk. When setbacks happen, the mind is often flooded with doubts: *I'm not good enough* or *I'll never recover.* Resilient people recognize these voices but refuse to let them define their reality. Instead, they intentionally replace discouragement with truth and encouragement. Saying to themselves, *This is hard, but I can grow through it*, or *I may have failed today, but tomorrow gives me another chance*, creates a mental framework that fuels perseverance rather than defeat.

Mental toughness is also strengthened by patience. Many quit not because they lack ability, but because they tire of waiting for results. Learning to endure seasons of waiting builds a resilience that shortcuts cannot offer. Think of a farmer planting seeds. There is no overnight harvest. The waiting can feel long, but patience is part of the process. In the same way, those who persevere mentally learn to see waiting not as wasted time, but as preparation for the reward to come.

Finally, building mental toughness requires perspective. People who endure difficulties well are often those who step back and see the bigger picture. Instead of viewing failure as the end, they see it as a lesson. Instead of focusing only on today's pain, they remember that challenges often lead to growth tomorrow. This perspective acts like a compass, guiding them through storms without losing direction. When the mind is trained to focus on purpose rather than problems, resilience becomes not just possible, but inevitable.

Strengthening Character Through Challenges

Challenges are more than obstacles—they are classrooms where character is tested, refined, and strengthened. While success often reveals our skills, adversity reveals our values. It is easy to appear disciplined, kind, or patient when life flows smoothly. However, when plans collapse, finances become tight, or relationships strain, our true character is revealed. In those moments, challenges serve as mirrors, revealing who we really are and giving us the opportunity to grow into who we want to be.

Character is not built in comfort—it is shaped in difficulty. A person who endures hardship learns humility by realizing they cannot control everything. They develop empathy because pain makes them more sensitive to others' struggles. They discover integrity through trials, which force them to choose between shortcuts and principles. In this sense, every challenge carries a hidden invitation to either become bitter and hardened or more refined and steadfast. Those who embrace the refining process discover virtues that last long after the trial has ended.

One of the most powerful ways challenges strengthen character is by teaching responsibility. When setbacks come, it is tempting to blame circumstances or other people. But true resilience takes ownership. We ask ourselves, *What can I learn? How can I grow?* This shift in perspective transforms challenges from punishments into opportunities. For example, someone who loses a job may feel crushed, but by owning their response—upgrading skills, networking, and persevering—they often discover doors they never would have considered before.

Another dimension of character shaped through challenges is perseverance in integrity. Pressure often tempts people to compromise—whether it's bending the truth, cutting corners, or abandoning values for short-term gain. Yet those who hold to their principles even when it costs them something emerge with a stronger sense of self. A person who refuses to cheat during tough times learns that real success is not about quick wins but about long-term faithfulness. Integrity tested under pressure becomes integrity proven.

Finally, challenges deepen gratitude and contentment. Those of us who have walked through valleys often appreciate the mountaintop moments more deeply. Scarcity makes abundance sweeter. Loss makes love richer. Failure makes achievement more meaningful.

By learning to value what we still have in the midst of difficulty, we strengthen a character that is not shaken by circumstances but grounded in perspective. In this way, challenges become not just burdens but blessings— stepping stones to maturity and wisdom.

Finding Hope and Purpose Amid Trials

Every trial has the power to either break us down or build us up. The difference lies in whether we can see beyond the immediate pain to the greater purpose it might serve. Hope is what keeps us from giving up when the weight of life feels unbearable. It whispers that today's struggle does not define tomorrow's outcome. Purpose transforms suffering into significance, reminding us that what we endure can shape not only our story but also the lives of those we influence.

In times of difficulty, it is easy to ask ourselves, *Why me?* Yet a more empowering question is, *What can I learn from this?* Hope does not erase hardship, but it reframes it as part of a larger journey. For example, a person who endures financial hardship may later use their experience to teach others about wise stewardship. Someone who overcomes illness may become an encouragement to those still battling. Purpose often grows out of pain, and it gives trials a meaning that makes them worth enduring.

Hope also anchors us when circumstances feel uncertain. Imagine a sailor caught in a storm. Without an anchor, the ship drifts aimlessly, at the mercy of the waves. But with an anchor, it holds steady, even if the storm rages on. In the same way, hope grounds us. It does not always calm the storm, but it keeps us steady until the waters settle. By clinging to hope, we train our hearts to see beyond the storm to the brighter days ahead.

Purpose further strengthens resilience by connecting our trials to a mission greater than ourselves. A parent may persevere through challenges because they want to leave a better future for their children. A leader may push forward in adversity because they know others depend on their example. When life is seen through the lens of service, setbacks lose some of their sting. They are no longer meaningless frustrations but part of a legacy being built step by step.

Finally, finding hope and purpose amid trials allows us to live with courage and faith. Challenges no longer become moments to fear but opportunities to demonstrate strength and endurance. Each time we rise from a fall, we testify that the human spirit is stronger than the obstacle. Each time we choose purpose over despair, we shine as examples to others who may be walking their own dark valleys. Hope keeps the heart alive, and purpose gives the journey direction; together, they turn trials into testimonies of resilience and perseverance.

Rising Stronger Every Time

Resilience and perseverance are not qualities reserved for the extraordinary—they are choices available to every one of us, every single day. Life will test us, sometimes with gentle nudges and other times with storms that feel impossible to survive. Yet each test carries within it the seed of strength, the chance to grow tougher, wiser, and more grounded. The question is not whether challenges will come—they surely will—but whether we will let them defeat us or define us.

Throughout this chapter, we have seen how resilience grows through emotional adaptability, mental toughness, character shaped by hardship, and the ability to find hope and purpose in trials. These are not abstract ideas, but practical truths lived out in the everyday grind of life. When a job is lost, when a plan fails, when a relationship cracks—these moments become opportunities to rise. Every setback, if met with perseverance, can be transformed into a setup for a greater comeback.

Resilience is not about never falling—it is about refusing to stay down. It is about training the mind to endure, the heart to hope, and the spirit to believe that tomorrow can still be better. Perseverance is the steady rhythm of progress—one step at a time, one day at a time—no matter how slow. Those who endure discover a strength they never thought they had, and in that strength lies the foundation of lasting success and happiness.

The truth is that your trials are not wasted. Every challenge you overcome builds a story of courage that inspires others. Every storm you endure without giving up makes you better able to guide someone else through theirs. In this way, resilience is not just personal—it becomes a communal quality. Your perseverance can be the light that helps someone else find their way through the dark.

So, when life presses hard against you, remember this: you were made to rise. The setback in front of you is not the end of your story but the beginning of a new chapter. Keep standing, keep moving, keep believing. Resilience and perseverance are the bridges that carry you from where you are to where you are meant to be. And when you cross that bridge, you will not only find success—you will find strength, character, and the unshakable joy that comes from never giving up.

CHAPTER 8

PRINCIPLE 8: CONTRIBUTION AND SERVICE – LIVING BEYOND YOURSELF

"A generous person will prosper; whoever refreshes others will be refreshed."—Proverbs 11:25

There is a profound truth woven into the fabric of life: happiness multiplies when it is shared. We live in a culture that often measures success by what we accumulate; yet, the greatest fulfillment rarely comes from holding on, but from giving. A person can achieve financial wealth, climb the career ladder, or reach personal milestones, but if their journey ends with themselves, something vital will always be missing. True joy is found not in what we hold on to, but in what we pour into the lives of others.

Contribution and service expand our vision beyond personal gain. They invite us to see our time, talents, and resources as tools to create impact. When we serve others, we become part of something greater than ourselves, something that echoes beyond our own lifespan. A kind word to someone discouraged, mentoring a young leader, or giving generously to those in need may seem small, but such acts ripple outward in ways we cannot fully see. They build legacies that no amount of self-centered achievement can replace.

Service also reshapes the way we see success. Instead of chasing recognition, we begin to measure our lives by the difference we make. A teacher may not earn millions, but the lives they inspire ripple forward for generations to come. A parent's sacrifices may never be publicly acknowledged, but they lay the foundation for future strength and stability. By serving, we tap into a deeper fulfillment that outlasts applause, achievements, or material possessions.

This principle is not about neglecting our own growth— it's about aligning our growth with purpose. The more we strengthen ourselves, the more we can offer to others. Just as a tree grows tall, providing shade, fruit, and shelter, our growth equips us to serve more effectively. Contribution and service are not drains on success—they are the very expression of it. To live beyond yourself is to live a life that leaves the world richer, warmer, and better because you were here.

In this chapter, we will explore the power of service through several dimensions: finding purpose in giving, serving with your unique gifts, the joy of generosity, service in relationships and community, and the lasting legacy of a life lived for others. Together, these themes will show us that the path to true happiness is not one we walk alone—it is one paved with compassion, generosity, and impact.

Finding Purpose in Giving

Over the years, Jean Luc has discovered that giving has a way of bringing clarity to life. There were seasons when he focused solely on personal goals: climbing ladders, meeting deadlines, and chasing milestones. Yet even when those goals were reached, the fulfillment didn't always match the effort. It wasn't until he began giving his time and energy to others that he realized something more profound was missing: purpose.

One example that stays with Jean Luc comes from volunteering with a local nonprofit that distributed food to families in need. At first, it felt like a small gesture, just a few hours each week. But when he stood across from parents relieved to have a meal for their children, or elders who didn't have to worry about their next plate of food, he realized he was touching lives in a way that had nothing to do with personal achievement. That experience reshaped his perspective. Giving wasn't just about charity—it was about seeing humanity more clearly and recognizing the value he could offer beyond himself.

This lesson has also been evident in everyday moments. At Amazon, as an Area Manager, Jean Luc has noticed how simply encouraging an associate or listening when someone is struggling can make a lasting difference. These acts, though small, build trust, inspire motivation, and remind us that leadership is fundamentally about service. When we measure work not only by productivity but by the positive impact on others, it creates deeper meaning and fulfillment.

Another powerful experience comes from Jean Luc's journey during the 2010 earthquake in Haiti. Like so many others, he faced challenges and losses that could have left him broken. Yet in the midst of that crisis, helping others—whether by sharing food, offering comfort, or simply being present—gave him renewed strength. Serving became a way to heal. In giving, he found hope; in serving, he discovered resilience.

What Jean Luc has learned is that giving doesn't diminish us—it extends us. Every act of generosity, no matter how small, connects us to something larger than our individual struggles. It shifts the focus from *What can I get? to What can I give?* In that shift, life becomes richer. Purpose is not just about personal success—it's about knowing that the world is better because we chose to give a part of ourselves to it.

Serving with Your Unique Gifts

One of the most freeing lessons Jean Luc has learned is that service is not about doing what everyone else does—it's about offering what only you can bring. Each of us has unique gifts, shaped by our experiences, talents, and even our struggles. For years, Jean Luc thought contribution meant grand gestures or financial giving.

However, he discovered that the greatest impact often comes from leaning into the abilities and insights God has already placed within us—a lesson Judlie has also come to embrace through her own journey of helping others.

For Jean Luc, one of those gifts has been leadership. In his role at Amazon, he doesn't just see tasks or quotas—he sees people. He has learned that one of his gifts is the ability to organize, motivate, and guide a team toward a common goal. There are days when associates come to work discouraged or stressed by life outside the warehouse. Taking time to encourage them, to speak life into them, or to show that they matter beyond their productivity is a way Jean Luc can serve using the gift of leadership.

Similarly, Judlie has found her unique way to serve through her ability to connect with people and provide guidance with empathy. Whether it's mentoring a young professional, offering support to a friend navigating challenges, or leading community initiatives, Judlie has discovered that listening, encouraging, and empowering others can be as impactful as any grand gesture. Together, we have learned that service is most meaningful when it reflects the gifts God has given each of us.

Jean Luc has also discovered this truth through his writing journey. For a long time, he didn't see his voice as a gift. But as he began writing this book, he realized that sharing his experiences, lessons, and faith could serve people in ways he might never be able to reach in person. Words have power—they can heal, challenge, inspire, and guide.

Judlie shares a similar insight from her own experiences. She has found that offering her perspective, encouragement, and practical guidance through conversation or mentoring allows her to serve others in ways that leave a lasting impact. Together, we recognize that service can take many forms—sometimes it is visible and tangible, and other times quiet and relational—but its effect is always profound.

Another example comes from Jean Luc's roots in Haiti. Growing up in an environment where resources were scarce, he developed creativity and problem-solving skills early. Those same skills, born out of necessity, became tools he could now use to help others. Judlie also draws strength from her background and life experiences, using her insights and compassion to uplift those around her. Whether it's teaching resilience, encouraging wise choices, or simply showing that someone cares, both of us view our unique experiences as gifts that enable us to provide meaningful service.

The beauty of serving with your gifts is that it doesn't drain you—it energizes you. When you serve in alignment with what you were uniquely designed to do, it feels natural, meaningful, and sustainable. That's the sweet spot where service is not a burden, but a joy. And when we each bring our unique gifts to the table, we create a fuller picture of what actual contribution looks like—a principle that guides both our personal lives and the message of this book.

The Joy of Generosity

Generosity has a way of unlocking joy that nothing else can. Jean Luc remembers the first time he gave, not out of obligation, but from a genuine desire to help. It wasn't a large sum of money or a grand display—it was something simple, like sharing food and clothes with a family in need. What surprised him most was how it made him feel. Instead of feeling like he had less, it gave him more—more joy, more gratitude, and a deeper sense of connection to others.

Judlie shares a similar experience from her own journey. She recalls moments of quietly helping someone in her community, offering guidance, encouragement, or support during a challenging time. Even small gestures, she found, carried profound meaning. The joy didn't come from recognition, but from knowing she had made a positive difference in another person's life.

Over the years, Jean Luc has come to realize that generosity isn't about the size of the gift, but the spirit behind it. Some of his happiest moments have come from mentoring a young associate at work, supporting a friend through a difficult period, or offering a financial blessing when he saw someone in need. Each act of generosity reminded him that happiness grows when it is shared.

Judlie has experienced this same truth. Whether helping a neighbor navigate a tough situation, volunteering for a local initiative, or simply giving her time to listen and encourage, she has discovered that giving creates a ripple effect—touching lives in ways that often extend far beyond the initial act. Together, we see that generosity not only transforms those who receive but also those who give.

Generosity also shifts how we view what we have. Jean Luc has learned that holding tightly to possessions or achievements breeds fear and anxiety, while opening hands to give invites peace and joy. Judlie has found that the practice of giving strengthens gratitude and perspective, revealing the abundance already present in life and highlighting opportunities to bless others in ways beyond material means.

The Bible says, "It is more blessed to give than to receive" (Acts 20:35), and both of us have experienced that truth firsthand. Generosity is not just about blessing others— it's about allowing God to work through us, filling our lives with a joy and fulfillment that money alone cannot buy.

Service in Relationships and Community

Service is not only about what we do for strangers—it begins with the people closest to us. Jean Luc has seen how serving within relationships—whether family, friends, or coworkers—creates bonds that grow deeper over time. True love, after all, is shown not just in words but in consistent actions of care, sacrifice, and presence.

Judlie has experienced this as well. For her, service often means setting aside her own plans to support loved ones, listening deeply when someone needs to talk, or providing encouragement during difficult seasons. These small acts—a meal prepared, a kind word, a moment of presence—build trust and create lasting connections in ways that words alone cannot.

At home, Jean Luc practices service by showing up faithfully for his family, celebrating milestones, and providing support during challenging times. He has learned that even small, intentional actions of care strengthen the bonds that hold relationships together.

In the community, service expands to a broader circle. Jean Luc has witnessed the strength that comes when people come together to serve, whether during the earthquake in Haiti or in local initiatives in the United States. Community service is more than just helping—it creates unity, reminds us that we are not alone, and allows people to overcome obstacles together.

Judlie also contributes to her community in meaningful ways, offering her time, guidance, and encouragement to those in need. Whether volunteering, mentoring, or supporting neighborhood efforts, she has discovered that consistent service can spark a ripple effect of kindness, bringing people together and strengthening connections.

In the workplace, Jean Luc emphasizes service by fostering teamwork and ensuring no one feels invisible or left behind. He celebrates wins together and supports colleagues through challenges. Judlie notes that when service is practiced in groups, it becomes contagious—one person's kindness inspires another, creating a culture of support and collaboration.

Relationships and community thrive when service is at the center. As we both have learned, serving in these spaces doesn't just bless others—it enriches our own lives, giving us a deeper sense of belonging, purpose, and fulfillment.

The Lasting Legacy of a Life Lived for Others

When we reach the end of our days, people will not remember us for the cars we drove, the titles we held, or the money in our bank accounts. They will remember how we made them feel, how we showed up, and how we served. A life lived for others leaves ripples that extend far beyond our lifetime. Those ripples become our legacy.

Jean Luc often reflects on his time in Haiti following the 2010 earthquake. Amid the rubble, despair, and loss, he witnessed acts of service that left a lasting impression. Strangers shared the little food they had, neighbors carried each other's burdens, and communities stood together to rebuild what had been lost. Many of those people didn't have wealth or influence by the world's standards, but they lived with a spirit of giving that created hope for generations to come. That, he realized, is what legacy looks like.

Judlie has seen this principle in her own life as well. In her community and family, she has found that consistent acts of care—helping a neighbor, mentoring a young person, or simply being present for someone in need—create a quiet but lasting impact. These moments may seem small at the time, but their effect extends far beyond what we can measure. Together, we have learned that legacy is built not in grand gestures alone, but in countless small choices to serve others with love.

In our own families, workplaces, and communities, we want those around us to remember us not just as people who worked hard, but as people who cared deeply. People who encouraged, lifted, and served others to reach higher. Legacy is not a single act—it is the sum of decisions made day by day to live generously, to walk humbly, and to place the needs of others alongside our own.

The beautiful truth is that legacy isn't about perfection. It's about direction—choosing to live each day with service as your compass. Jean Luc and Judlie have both discovered that when service is motivated by love, the impact multiplies far beyond what we could ever anticipate. People may forget our words, but they will never forget the warmth of our actions.

Jesus Himself said, "Whoever wants to be great among you must be your servant" (Matthew 20:26). That greatness is not found in accolades but in a life poured out for others. When we embrace contribution and service as the heart of our journey, we leave behind something more valuable than wealth. We leave inspiration, love, and hope for the next generation.

A life lived for others is never wasted—it is the richest life of all.

The Fulfilled Life of Service

At the heart of true happiness and success lies a principle that the world often overlooks: the value of contribution and service. Achievements fade, possessions lose their shine, and even milestones eventually become memories. However, the impact of a life dedicated to serving others endures, shaping hearts, building communities, and inspiring change long after we are gone.

Service transforms us from the inside out. When we give our time, talents, and resources, we discover a more profound sense of purpose than anything self-centered living can provide. We shift from asking ourselves, *What can I gain?* to asking, *What can I give?* That shift changes everything—our priorities, our relationships, and even our definition of success.

The truth is, serving doesn't always require grand gestures. It may look like mentoring someone younger in your field, lending a hand to a struggling neighbor, or taking time to really listen to a friend in need. These everyday acts of kindness carry immeasurable weight, and they often become the moments people remember most. Small seeds of service grow into legacies of love.

When you live beyond yourself, you also unlock a joy that cannot be found anywhere else. Generosity releases you from the grip of selfishness, comparison, and emptiness. It replaces them with peace, gratitude, and a sense of belonging to something bigger than yourself. Serving is not a sacrifice that drains—it's an investment that multiplies.

So, ask yourself, *What kind of legacy am I building?* Your career, accomplishments, and possessions are tools, but service is the true story they should tell. A life of giving ensures that your influence will not end with you—it will continue to shape the lives of those you touched, creating ripples that extend into the future.

As we carry this principle forward, let us remember that happiness shared is happiness multiplied, and a life of service is a life that never truly ends. To live beyond yourself is to live fully, deeply, and meaningfully. That is the path to success that lasts forever.

CHAPTER 9

PRINCIPLE 9: INTEGRITY AND CHARACTER – THE FOUNDATION OF TRUST

"The integrity of the upright guides them, but the unfaithful are destroyed by their duplicity."—Proverbs 11:3

Skills, talent, and accomplishments may open doors, but they are not enough to sustain a meaningful life. Without integrity and strong character, even the most successful achievements can crumble under scrutiny or ethical failure. True happiness, influence, and long-term success are rooted not in what you can achieve but in who you are when no one is watching. Integrity is the compass that guides every decision, shapes every relationship, and protects every opportunity you earn.

Character is tested in the small moments as much as in the grand ones. A choice to speak honestly, even when a lie would be easier, builds trust that cannot be bought. A decision to follow through on a promise, even when inconvenient, strengthens relationships that last a lifetime. In our own journeys, we've seen how consistently acting with integrity transforms the way people respond to you, whether in the workplace, at home, or in the community. People may forget what you said, but they will always remember whether you were trustworthy.

Integrity is not just a moral compass; it is also a stabilizer for life's challenges. When crises arise, those who have consistently acted with honesty and ethical behavior can navigate them with confidence and clarity. They do not crumble under pressure or fear exposure—they have built a foundation strong enough to withstand scrutiny, setbacks, and misunderstandings. By cultivating character, we create a life that cannot be easily shaken by external circumstances.

In a world that often rewards shortcuts and compromise, choosing integrity can feel like swimming against the current. Yet every decision to honor honesty, authenticity, and fairness compounds over time. Like a tree whose roots grow deep in fertile soil, a life grounded in strong character withstands storms and continues to flourish. The respect and trust earned through integrity are not temporary—they form a legacy that impacts families, communities, and future generations.

This chapter will explore how integrity and character manifest in various areas of life, including personal accountability, ethical decision-making, honesty in communication, the courage to stand firm in our values, and the long-term rewards of living authentically.

Through stories, examples, and practical insights, we will see why character is not just an admirable trait— it is the foundation on which all lasting success and fulfillment are built.

Ethical Decision-Making in Everyday Life

Ethics is not just a concept for boardrooms or legal codes—it is the daily practice of making choices that align with values, fairness, and honesty. Early in his career, Jean Luc faced situations where shortcuts or bending rules seemed tempting. On one occasion, a process could have been expedited by overlooking a safety protocol. While it would have saved time and earned temporary praise, Jean Luc chose to follow the proper procedure. That decision delayed results but reinforced a culture of integrity, safety, and accountability that ultimately strengthened the entire team.

Ethical decision-making often comes down to small choices repeated consistently over time. For example, both of us have learned to respond truthfully to questions, even when the answer might make others uncomfortable, and to address conflicts with clarity rather than avoidance. These may seem minor in isolation, but over time, they create a pattern of trustworthiness. People notice when you consistently act in alignment with your principles, and that reliability becomes one of your most valuable assets.

One story that stands out involved a financial decision in a business project. There was an opportunity to cut corners and reduce expenses, which would have inflated short-term profits. However, Jean Luc recognized that doing so would have compromised honesty with clients and potentially harmed long-term credibility. Choosing the principled path required courage, and the immediate benefits were not as visible, yet the long-term results reinforced relationships, trust, and the reputation of integrity we were building.

Ethical decision-making also extends to how we treat others. It is choosing fairness over favoritism, respect over expedience, and transparency over manipulation. In daily interactions—whether mentoring a junior colleague, negotiating contracts, or even responding to simple requests—our ethical choices accumulate into a reputation that precedes us. That reputation becomes a foundation of influence and leadership that cannot be bought or faked.

Finally, ethics is not about rigid rules or external enforcement—it is a reflection of character. The decisions we make daily define us more than any public recognition or achievement. By prioritizing integrity in our choices, we create a life that is dependable, honorable, and inspiring, fostering trust in every relationship and endeavor.

Honesty in Communication and Influence

Communication is one of the most powerful tools we have to shape relationships, build trust, and lead effectively. Yet its power is only as strong as the honesty behind it. Early in his career, Jean Luc noticed how quickly misinformation or half-truths could create tension and confusion within a team. Through experience, we both learned that speaking honestly, even when the truth is uncomfortable, is far more effective than trying to smooth things over with vague words or omissions.

One specific experience stands out. Jean Luc was leading a project with tight deadlines, and a mistake in planning threatened to delay the outcome. Instead of hiding it or assigning blame, he chose to communicate openly with his team and leadership. He explained the situation, took responsibility, and shared a plan to rectify the issue. The result was remarkable. Not only did the team solve the problem more quickly, but the trust within the group also strengthened. That moment reinforced what we both believe—that honesty can transform a potential breakdown into an opportunity for collaboration and growth.

Influence is built on credibility, and credibility is rooted in truthfulness. We have found that when people know they can rely on your word, they are far more willing to follow, support, and cooperate with you. In both professional and personal settings, influence is not solely about authority or persuasion—it is earned by consistently communicating with integrity. When your words align with your actions, your influence multiplies naturally.

Honesty in communication also requires courage and humility. It may involve admitting mistakes, expressing difficult feedback, or setting boundaries that others may initially resist. Jean Luc remembers guiding a junior colleague who had struggled with meeting expectations. He chose to be honest about the areas that needed improvement while also affirming the colleague's potential. That balance of truth and encouragement created accountability without breaking morale—an approach we both continue to value in leadership and mentorship.

Finally, honesty fosters authenticity, inspiring loyalty, and deepening connections. People are drawn to those who are honest, transparent, and trustworthy. In every conversation, decision, or presentation, honesty acts as the bridge between our character and our impact. By consistently communicating with truth, we build influence that lasts, relationships that endure, and a life that reflects the integrity we value.

Courage to Stand Firm in Your Values

Courage is not the absence of fear but the decision to hold firm when compromise feels easier. Standing by your values requires strength in moments when everything around you urges flexibility. It is the inner resolve to prioritize what is right over what is convenient. This kind of courage becomes the backbone of integrity, allowing you to remain consistent even when the stakes are high.

When challenges arise, the temptation to bend or adjust your values for comfort or gain can be strong. Yet it is in those very moments that your true character is revealed. Every decision either strengthens or weakens your integrity. By remaining faithful to your principles, you cultivate a moral consistency that becomes unshakable over time.

Courageous living also protects you from regret. When your choices align with your deepest convictions, you carry no burden of compromise. Even if the outcome is difficult, you can stand with confidence, knowing your actions were anchored in truth. This assurance fosters a deep sense of peace because you have acted with alignment rather than contradiction.

Ultimately, the courage to stand firm in your values is what builds trust. People respect consistency, even when they may disagree with your decisions. By showing unwavering commitment to what is right, you demonstrate reliability and authenticity. That strength inspires others and reinforces your own path of integrity.

The Long-Term Rewards of Living Authentically

Living authentically is more than a momentary decision; it is a way of life that shapes every aspect of your future. Authenticity aligns your actions with your inner convictions, ensuring that who you are in private matches who you are in public. Over time, this consistency produces stability, peace, and a freedom that appearances or shortcuts cannot manufacture.

The long-term rewards of authenticity include the ability to move forward without the burden of pretense. When you no longer waste energy maintaining false impressions, you can focus entirely on growth, purpose, and contribution. This clarity frees you to pursue goals with confidence, knowing you are not building success on shaky foundations.

Authenticity also creates lasting influence. A genuine person attracts trust and respect, and that trust compounds over the years. Unlike fleeting achievements or temporary recognition, the credibility that comes from authentic living leaves an enduring mark. This is the kind of reputation that sustains opportunities and deepens meaningful connections.

In the end, living authentically leads to wholeness. It ensures that double standards or hidden contradictions do not fragment your life. Instead, your values, words, and actions align, creating harmony both internally and externally. Such a life may not always be the easiest path, but it is always the most rewarding—one that leaves behind peace, respect, and a legacy of truth.

The Enduring Strength of Integrity

Integrity and character are the quiet forces that give true meaning to success. They are not just values to admire, but disciplines to live by daily. When your actions align with your convictions, you cultivate trust, stability, and inner peace that no achievement can provide on its own.

The journey of success is filled with opportunities, challenges, and choices. What determines whether it endures is not how much you accomplish, but how faithfully you uphold your principles along the way. Integrity turns fleeting victories into lasting fulfillment.

Let your life be anchored in honesty, guided by authenticity, and strengthened by unwavering character. For in the end, it is not only what you achieve that will be remembered, but who you became in the process.

As we close our exploration of integrity and character, it becomes clear that living authentically is more than just making the right choices—it is about aligning every part of our lives with values that endure. Yet even a strong character needs direction. Without a more profound sense of purpose, our integrity can feel like a compass with no map. That is why the journey now leads us to the final principle: grounding our lives in purpose and faith. These anchors not only give meaning to our actions but also sustain us when success, happiness, and trials all test the core of who we are.

CHAPTER 10

PRINCIPLE 10: PURPOSE AND FAITH – ANCHORS FOR A MEANINGFUL LIFE

"For I know the plans I have for you," declares the Lord, "plans to prosper you and not to harm you, plans to give you hope and a future." —Jeremiah 29:11

A life without purpose often feels like wandering in a desert—busy, active, but without direction. Success alone cannot fill the void, nor can possessions or titles provide lasting fulfillment. True meaning comes when you anchor yourself to something greater than personal ambition. Purpose gives clarity to your choices, and faith sustains you when challenges arise. Together, they form the foundation of a life that is both meaningful and enduring.

In today's fast-moving world, it is easy to chase goals that look impressive but feel empty once achieved. Without purpose, we risk building lives that shine on the outside yet lack peace within. Faith provides a steady anchor in this chaos, reminding us that we are not accidents of chance but part of a greater design. It connects our everyday actions to a higher calling and reassures us that setbacks and struggles can still serve a divine purpose.

Purpose and faith also bring balance to the tension between striving and surrender. While ambition pushes us forward, faith teaches us to rest in trust, knowing that not everything is under our control. This balance is liberating because it allows us to work diligently without being enslaved by anxiety or fear of failure. In this way, faith doesn't stifle effort—it fuels it with hope and direction.

When purpose and faith intertwine, life becomes more than a series of tasks and achievements. Every decision, relationship, and accomplishment gains deeper meaning. Instead of asking ourselves, *What do I want to achieve?*, the question shifts to, *How does this align with my greater purpose?* That shift changes everything—it brings peace in storms, joy in service, and hope even in uncertainty.

Discovering Your True North

Every journey needs a direction, and every life needs a compass. Your true north is that inner sense of purpose that keeps you aligned with what truly matters, even when life's winds shift or distractions pull you off course. It's not something you invent—it's something you uncover through reflection, faith, and intentional living. Many people spend their lives chasing goals that seem urgent but never fulfill them, only to realize later that they've been climbing the wrong mountain. Discovering your true north is about aligning your life with meaning, not just motion.

This discovery often begins in moments of stillness. When you slow down long enough to listen, the noise of the world fades, and the voice within becomes clearer. Purpose doesn't shout—it whispers. It calls you through your passions, your values, and your desire to make a difference. Faith acts as the compass that points you toward that calling, especially when you feel lost or uncertain. It reminds you that your life is part of a divine plan that is still unfolding.

True purpose also grows through experience. Sometimes, you find clarity not in success, but in struggle. The challenges you overcome often reveal your deepest strengths and the causes you were meant to serve. Purpose refines itself through both triumph and failure—each shaping your understanding of who you are and what you're here to do. It's in those moments of trial that faith gives purpose its staying power, turning pain into direction and confusion into conviction.

Many lose sight of their true north by confusing busyness with purpose. They run harder each day but feel emptier inside. The truth is, productivity without purpose is like rowing without a destination—you move, but you never arrive. Real direction begins when you pause to ask yourself more profound questions: *Why am I doing this? Who am I serving? What legacy am I building?* Purpose provides answers that money, success, or status never can.

When you begin living guided by your true north, life takes on a new rhythm. You no longer chase after every opportunity. Instead, you choose the ones that align with your calling. You stop comparing your path to others because you understand that your journey is uniquely designed for you. Faith and purpose work together like the compass and the map—one shows direction, the other gives confidence in the route. And when those align, you not only find success—you find fulfillment.

Faith as the Anchor of Purpose

Purpose without faith is like a ship without an anchor—it drifts wherever the tides take it. Faith gives your purpose weight, stability, and meaning. It grounds your vision in something greater than yourself, reminding you that your life is part of a bigger story. When the storms of uncertainty rise, faith keeps you from being tossed by fear or doubt. It allows you to trust the process even when you can't see the destination.

Faith doesn't mean everything will go as planned—it means you believe there is a plan even when life doesn't go your way. Many times, your path will lead through seasons of waiting, loss, or disappointment. Without faith, those moments feel meaningless. But with faith, they become part of your preparation—strengthening your character and sharpening your vision. Faith teaches patience, humility, and resilience, revealing that setbacks often hold hidden blessings.

Anchoring your purpose in faith also helps you stay steady amid success. It's easy to lose perspective when achievements pile up and recognition comes your way. Faith reminds you that your abilities are gifts, not trophies. It shifts the focus from personal glory to service and gratitude. You begin to see success not as a symbol of self-importance but as an opportunity to bless others and fulfill a divine assignment.

Faith also transforms how you handle uncertainty. When life's answers are delayed or unclear, faith gives you the courage to move forward step by step. You learn to walk not by sight but by conviction. This posture allows you to make peace with the unknown, trusting that what's unseen is often where God is working most. In those moments, faith becomes not just your anchor but your light.

Ultimately, faith and purpose work together as a compass and a foundation. Faith gives purpose, direction; purpose gives faith expression. Together, they create a life that is deeply rooted yet continually growing—a life that weathers change, endures hardship, and inspires others. When faith anchors your purpose, your journey becomes more than a pursuit of success—it becomes an act of worship, an offering of your life to something eternal.

Living with Eternal Perspective

When life is viewed only through the lens of the present, challenges feel unbearable and success feels fleeting. But when you live with an eternal perspective, everything gains meaning. You begin to understand that life is not a sprint but a journey of preparation—for something greater, something beyond what eyes can see. This perspective changes how you react to hardship, how you handle success, and how you treat others along the way. You stop living just for the next achievement and start living for lasting impact.

An eternal perspective reminds you that your purpose is not limited to earthly success. Money, status, and possessions will fade, but the love, kindness, and faith you sow in others will echo beyond your lifetime. When your heart is anchored in eternity, you prioritize what truly matters: relationships, integrity, compassion, and spiritual growth. Numbers or trophies cannot measure these things, but they form the legacy that outlives you. A life lived this way brings peace that no amount of achievement can buy.

This mindset also gives you strength in the face of suffering. When you face loss, rejection, or disappointment, faith reminds you that pain is not the end of your story. Every trial becomes a teacher, every setback a setup for transformation. You begin to view challenges not as evidence of abandonment but as moments of divine refinement. The eternal view lifts your eyes from what's temporary to what's timeless, teaching you to endure, trust, and keep moving forward with hope.

Living with an eternal perspective also changes how you spend your time. You become intentional with your days, knowing they are precious and limited. You seek to invest in what truly matters rather than waste energy on comparisons, grudges, or meaningless pursuits. Gratitude grows, contentment deepens, and every day becomes an opportunity to live with purpose. You realize that fulfillment doesn't come from doing more—it comes from living in alignment with what lasts forever.

An eternal perspective brings harmony between faith and purpose. It keeps your ambition grounded in humility and your progress rooted in peace. You understand that your greatest reward is not found in recognition but in the quiet satisfaction of knowing you lived faithfully and loved well. When your eyes are fixed on eternity, your steps on earth find clarity, strength, and meaning.

Purpose in Everyday Life

Purpose is not always found in grand missions or world-changing projects. More often, it's discovered in the small, consistent acts of meaning that shape your daily life. Many people spend years searching for a purpose that feels extraordinary, only to overlook the quiet significance of what they already do. Every conversation, every act of kindness, every effort to improve—even when unseen—can carry eternal weight. Purpose is not about doing something famous—it's about being faithful in whatever lies before you.

When you begin to live with this mindset, even ordinary days become sacred. The simple act of showing up—doing your work with integrity, caring for your family, encouraging a struggling friend—takes on deeper meaning. It's in those small, intentional choices that a life of impact is built. You may not always feel like you are making a difference, but purpose doesn't depend on emotion—it depends on alignment with your values. The truth is, greatness often hides in consistency, not recognition.

Living with purpose in everyday life also requires mindfulness. It means being present in each moment rather than rushing from one goal to the next. So many people live distracted, chasing what's next while missing what's now. But purpose flourishes when you slow down long enough to notice the opportunities in front of you. A word of encouragement, a thoughtful gesture, or a few minutes of listening can shift someone's entire day. Purpose is woven into these moments when your attention and heart are fully engaged.

True purpose also requires humility. It's easy to believe that meaning must come from significant achievements, but purpose is found wherever love is practiced.

Sometimes your greatest contribution will not be what you do, but who you are: how you treat people, how you handle adversity, and how you live your values when no one is watching. Each of these actions becomes a reflection of what you believe. Purpose is not discovered through striving—it's revealed through faithful living.

Finally, living with purpose every day brings deep satisfaction because it aligns your outer actions with your inner convictions. When your work, relationships, and choices all flow from the same source of truth, life begins to feel whole and complete. There's no longer a divide between who you are and what you do. Every day becomes a reflection of your calling, and even the smallest act can become a form of worship—a way to honor your Creator and contribute to something larger than yourself.

Living Fully and Finishing Well

To live fully is to live intentionally—to wake each day with gratitude, focus, and faith. A full life is not measured by the number of years you live, but by the depth of your purpose within them. Each sunrise offers a new opportunity to grow, to serve, and to reflect the light that has been placed within you. The people who finish well are not those who have had perfect journeys, but those who stayed faithful through imperfect moments. They keep moving forward even when progress feels slow because they understand that every season, whether bright or stormy, has meaning in the greater design of life.

Living fully means refusing to waste your days on distractions or regrets. It's choosing presence over pressure, and purpose over busyness. Many people chase after success only to realize they've climbed the wrong mountain. But when you anchor your life in purpose and faith, you climb with clarity. Every step becomes meaningful because it leads you toward something eternal. You begin to measure success not by wealth or fame but by peace, growth, and love—the true indicators of a life well-lived.

Finishing well requires endurance and perspective. It's easy to start strong when enthusiasm is high, but the real test comes in the middle, when the path feels long and the rewards seem distant. In those moments, faith becomes your strength. It reminds you that your journey is not in vain, and that perseverance produces maturity, wisdom, and unshakable peace. Finishing well means not giving up when it's hard, not losing heart when others don't understand, and trusting that your labor, done with integrity, will never be wasted.

A life of purpose also calls for peace with the past and hope for the future. You cannot live fully if you are chained by regret or bitterness. Forgive freely, release what you cannot change, and focus on what you can build today.

Each day is a gift, and every breath is an opportunity to do something that matters—to encourage, to uplift, to create, to love. The more you live this way, the more your days overflow with meaning and joy, even in the simplest moments.

To finish well is not to end perfectly, but to end faithfully. It's to look back and know you lived with courage, integrity, and compassion—that you made the world a little brighter and the people around you a little stronger. When faith becomes your foundation and purpose your compass, your life tells a story worth remembering. The greatest legacy is not what you leave behind, but what you build within—the love you shared, the people you inspired, and the unwavering light of hope that continues to shine long after you are gone.

CONCLUSION

BUILDING YOUR LIFE
OF SUCCESS AND HAPPINESS

Success and happiness are not destinations waiting at the end of the road—they are journeys we walk every day. They are shaped by the choices we make, the principles we live by, and the mindset we carry through both triumphs and trials. In a rapidly changing world, circumstances will shift, plans will evolve, and challenges will appear unexpectedly. Yet, one thing always remains within your control: how you choose to think, act, and respond.

Each of the ten principles in this book offers a building block for a meaningful life. Clarity of vision helps you see where you are going. Discipline and consistency keep you moving forward when motivation fades. Adaptability allows you to remain flexible without losing who you are. Emotional intelligence deepens your relationships, while a growth mindset keeps you learning and evolving. Balance guards your peace, resilience strengthens your spirit, and service opens your heart. Integrity grounds you in truth, and faith gives your life purpose beyond achievement.

Together, these principles form more than a guide—they create a way of living that honors both success and happiness as daily companions. When you live with intentionality, when your values direct your actions, and when your faith sustains your purpose, success becomes sustainable and joy becomes steady. You stop chasing fulfillment and start living it.

No one can predict the future, but you can prepare for it with the right foundation. These principles are not temporary strategies; they are timeless truths that empower you to lead with courage, act with wisdom, and live with compassion. When you practice them daily, you will discover that success is not measured merely by wealth or recognition, but by peace of mind, integrity of heart, and the positive impact you leave behind.

This is your blueprint. This is your moment. Choose to live with vision, discipline, adaptability, and faith, and you will not only build a life of success but one filled with meaning, peace, and lasting happiness.

ABOUT THE AUTHORS

Jean Luc Blanc and Judlie Pierre-Jacques are a husband-and-wife team whose lives reflect the very principles they share in this book—faith, perseverance, integrity, and service. Living in Silver Spring, Maryland, United States, they have built their lives around the belief that true success and happiness are achieved through purpose, discipline, and compassion for others.

Jean Luc holds a master's degree in business administration and brings extensive experience in leadership, strategy, and personal development. Judlie complements this with a strong background in the social sciences and business, along with a deep passion for empowering others through faith and personal growth. Together, they bring a powerful blend of leadership, empathy, and spiritual grounding to their work.

Their shared vision for *10 Principles for a Life of Success and Happiness* is to empower others to build meaningful, balanced, and purpose-driven lives—no matter where they start from. Through their writing, Jean Luc and Judlie hope to inspire readers to live with clarity, faith, and a commitment to personal and spiritual growth.